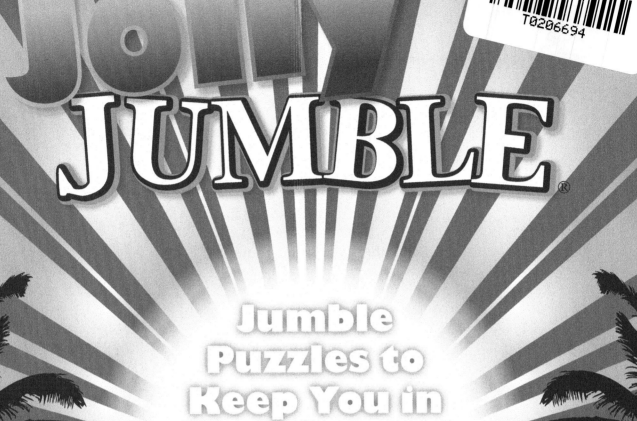

# JOLLY JUMBLE®

Jumble
Puzzles to
Keep You in
High Spirits!

Henri Arnold,
Bob Lee,
and
Mike Argirion

TRIUMPH
BOOKS

T0206694

Jumble® is a registered trademark
of Tribune Media Services, Inc.

Copyright © 2008 by Tribune Media Services, Inc.
All rights reserved.

This book is available in quantity at special discounts
for your group or organization.

For further information, contact:

**Triumph Books**
814 North Franklin Street
Chicago, Illinois 60610
(312) 337-0747
www.triumphbooks.com

Printed in U.S.A.

ISBN: 978-1-60078-214-5

Design by Sue Knopf

# CONTENTS

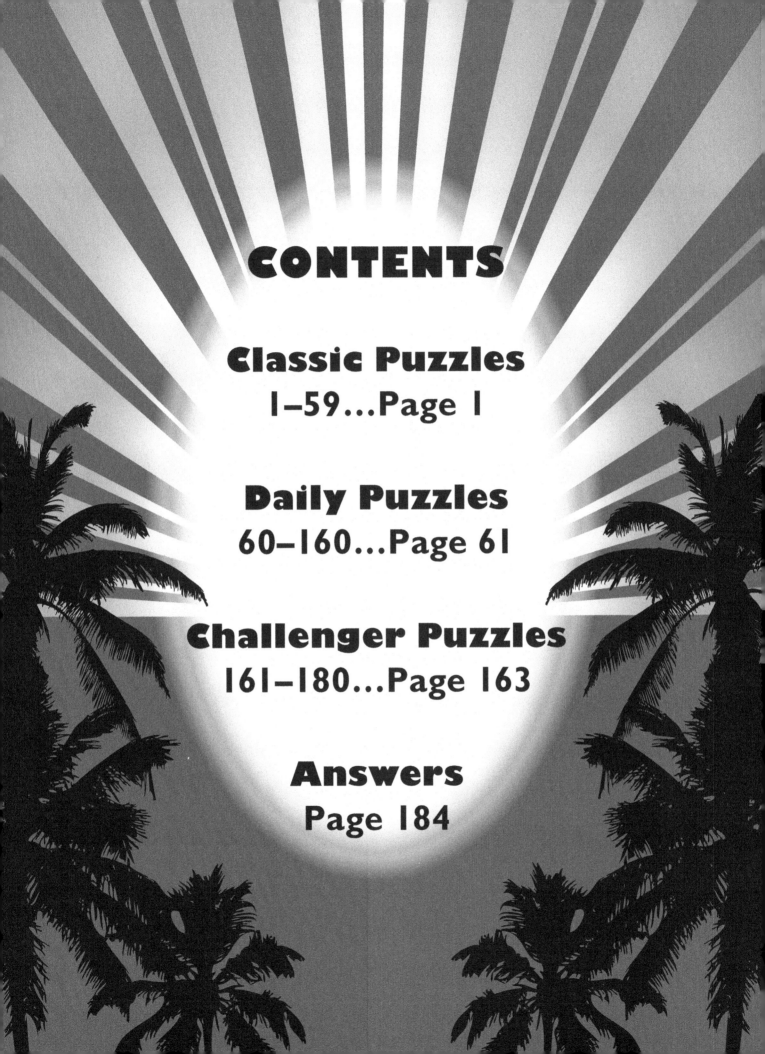

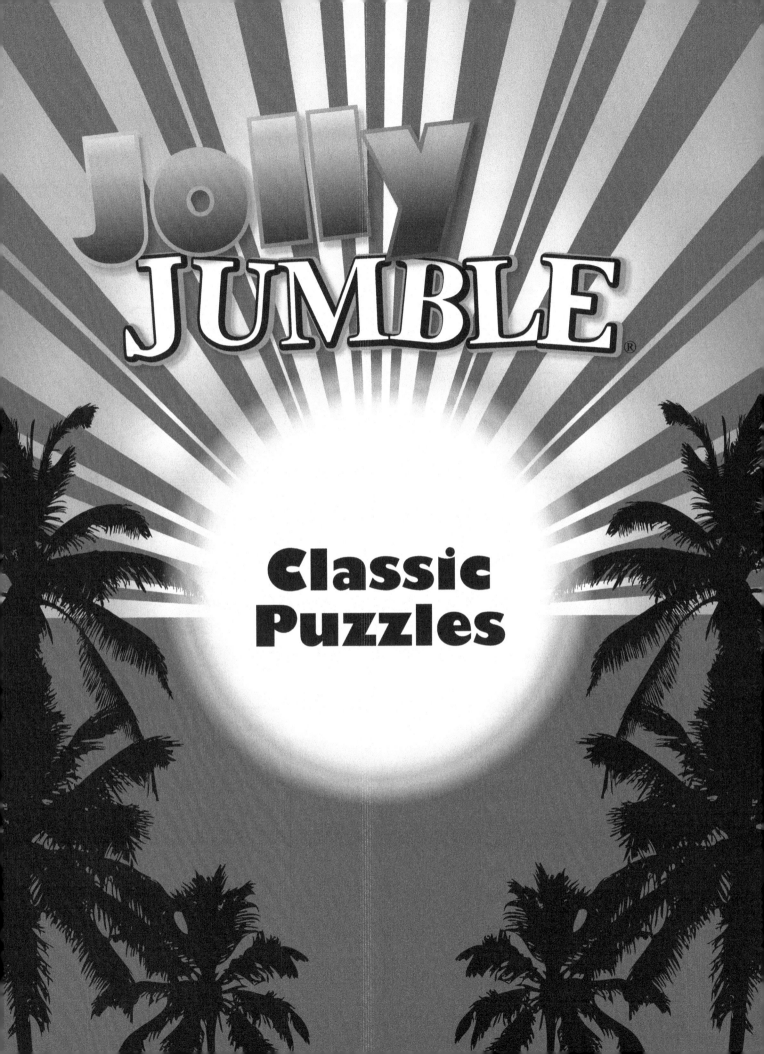

# JUMBLE®

Unscramble these four Jumbles, one letter to each square, to form four ordinary words.

**RONOC**

**NORST**

**DIMRAY**

**CHROID**

If she'll only say "yes"

WHAT A MAN SOMETIMES GETS FROM A WOMAN WHO LOOKS LIKE A DREAM.

Now arrange the circled letters to form the surprise answer, as suggested by the above cartoon.

**Print answer here**

# JUMBLE®

Unscramble these four Jumbles, one letter to each square, to form four ordinary words.

DULGI

ROAHB

THINGK

KNEBOC

I like a man who tells it to me straight

BACK TALK IS OFTEN MORE HONEST THAN THIS KIND OF TALK.

Now arrange the circled letters to form the surprise answer, as suggested by the above cartoon.

*Print answer here*

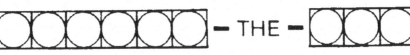

— THE —

# JUMBLE®

Unscramble these four Jumbles, one letter to each square, to form four ordinary words.

DRAIP

EMAHR

GLYNIK

CONTOY

THEY'RE COMPLAINING THAT THE LAMB IS TOUGH

Now arrange the circled letters to form the surprise answer, as suggested by the above cartoon.

*Print answer here* " LET'S NOT ⬡⬡⬡⬡ '⬡⬡⬡⬡ ' "

# JUMBLE®

Unscramble these four Jumbles, one letter to
each square, to form four ordinary words.

**YOLID**

**VREEV**

**TARYEW**

**NARXLY**

She'd better
watch her step

WHEN A WOMAN
"FISHES" FOR A
HUSBAND SHE
SHOULD KNOW THIS.

Now arrange the circled letters to form the
surprise answer, as suggested by the above
cartoon.

*Print
answer
here*  WHERE ◯◯◯ ◯◯◯◯ THE ◯◯◯◯

# JUMBLE®

Unscramble these four Jumbles, one letter to each square, to form four ordinary words.

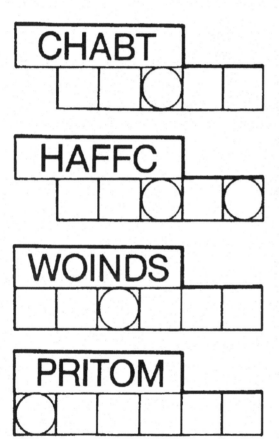

CHABT

HAFFC

WOINDS

PRITOM

SOMETIMES COMES TO A HEAD WHEN INSULTS ARE THROWN BACK AND FORTH.

Now arrange the circled letters to form the surprise answer, as suggested by the above cartoon.

*Print answer here*

# JUMBLE®

Unscramble these four Jumbles, one letter to
each square, to form four ordinary words.

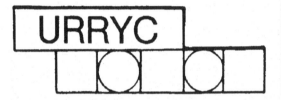
URRYC

BYBEA

MOPSIE

BOMERY

Never a bus
when you need one

WENT ON FOOT IN
A RAINSTORM.

Now arrange the circled letters to form the
surprise answer, as suggested by the above
cartoon.

Print answer here

# JUMBLE®

Unscramble these four Jumbles, one letter to each square, to form four ordinary words.

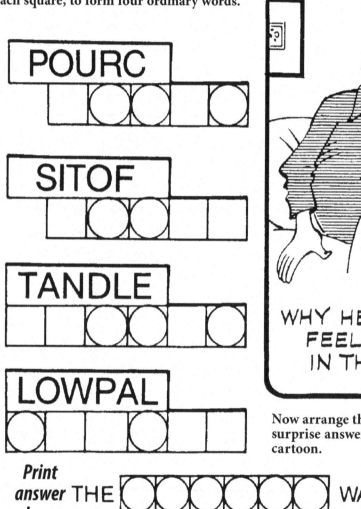

POURC

SITOF

TANDLE

LOWPAL

WHY HE WOKE UP FEELING DOWN IN THE MOUTH.

Now arrange the circled letters to form the surprise answer, as suggested by the above cartoon.

**Print answer here**  THE ⬡⬡⬡⬡⬡⬡ WAS ⬡⬡⬡⬡

Unscramble these four Jumbles, one letter to each square, to form four ordinary words.

FLYIM

JEDDA

CLOTEK

BELUBB

Look--I just ran into Sally--
She was my first girlfriend
before you came along

MIGHT SET OFF
AN EXPLOSION
IN THE HOME.

Now arrange the circled letters to form the surprise answer, as suggested by the above cartoon.

**Print answer here** AN ◯◯◯ ◯◯◯◯◯

# JUMBLE®

Unscramble these four Jumbles, one letter to
each square, to form four ordinary words.

HELAT

CHITH

GREESY

RIGDIF

SOMETIMES
THEY'RE A WOMAN'S
ARCH ENEMIES.

Now arrange the circled letters to form the
surprise answer, as suggested by the above
cartoon.

*Print answer here*  ⬡⬡⬡⬡ ⬡⬡⬡⬡⬡

# JUMBLE®

Unscramble these four Jumbles, one letter to
each square, to form four ordinary words.

REVNY

MOCEA

WEABER

ASHIMP

WHEN PRICES
"SOAR"---

Now arrange the circled letters to form the
surprise answer, as suggested by the above
cartoon.

*Print answer here*

11

# JUMBLE®

Unscramble these four Jumbles, one letter to each square, to form four ordinary words.

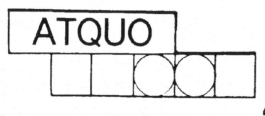

ATQUO

RUHTT

RUGBBY

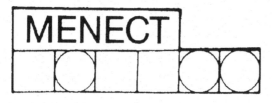

MENECT

WHAT THE ROULETTE WHEEL TOOK FOR A CHANGE.

Now arrange the circled letters to form the surprise answer, as suggested by the above cartoon.

Print answer here A ⬡⬡⬡⬡⬡ FOR THE "⬡⬡⬡⬡⬡⬡⬡"

# JUMBLE®

Unscramble these four Jumbles, one letter to each square, to form four ordinary words.

JEGUD

EMICH

NEXETT

CAVIDE

WHAT HAPPENED
WHEN FOUR COUPLES
WENT TO A
RESTAURANT?

Now arrange the circled letters to form the surprise answer, as suggested by the above cartoon.

*Print answer here*

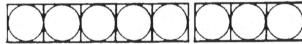

# JUMBLE®

Unscramble these four Jumbles, one letter to each square, to form four ordinary words.

LORBI

CUEJI

LOUGEY

BOOMAB

Shut up and keep chewing

WHAT LITTLE WHALES LIKE BEST.

Now arrange the circled letters to form the surprise answer, as suggested by the above cartoon.

*Print answer here* " ⭘⭘⭘⭘⭘⭘⭘ " ⭘⭘⭘

# JUMBLE®

Unscramble these four Jumbles, one letter to
each square, to form four ordinary words.

DORBO

TRIHM

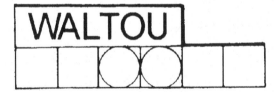

WALTOU

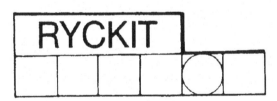

RYCKIT

Arf!

WHAT THEY CALLED
THE HARDWARE
STORE'S CAT.

Now arrange the circled letters to form the
surprise answer, as suggested by the above
cartoon.

*Print answer here* THE "  "

# JUMBLE®

Unscramble these four Jumbles, one letter to each square, to form four ordinary words.

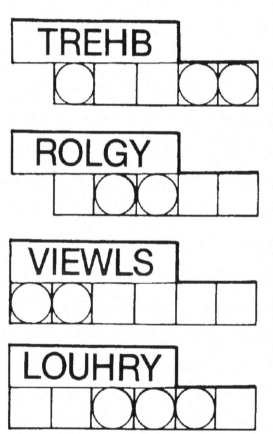

TREHB

ROLGY

VIEWLS

LOUHRY

WHAT THE RODEO PERFORMER DOES IN ORDER TO IMPRESS OTHERS.

Now arrange the circled letters to form the surprise answer, as suggested by the above cartoon.

**Print answer here** ◯◯◯◯◯◯ THE ◯◯◯◯

# JUMBLE®

Unscramble these four Jumbles, one letter to
each square, to form four ordinary words.

SEPOI

MIGRY

INCANE

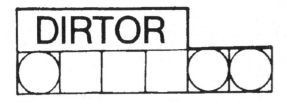

DIRTOR

Dear, it's your boss

HE WAS SO LAZY
HE WOULDN'T EVEN
EXERCISE THIS.

Now arrange the circled letters to form the
surprise answer, as suggested by the above
cartoon.

*Print answer here*

# JUMBLE®

Unscramble these four Jumbles, one letter to
each square, to form four ordinary words.

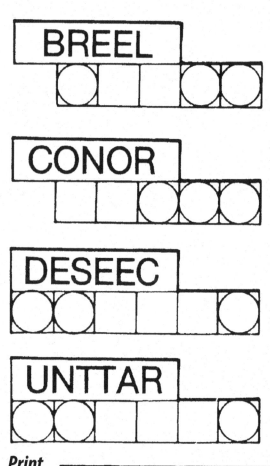

BREEL

CONOR

DESEEC

UNTTAR

WHEN WILL THE
MAIL ARRIVE?

Now arrange the circled letters to form the
surprise answer, as suggested by the above
cartoon.

*Print*
*answer*
*here*

OR ""

# JUMBLE®

Unscramble these four Jumbles, one letter to each square, to form four ordinary words.

RICOU

BYNAD

CARPHE

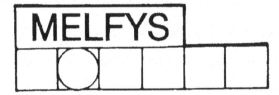

MELFYS

WHAT DRY-AS-DUST PEOPLE NEVER SEEM TO DO.

Now arrange the circled letters to form the surprise answer, as suggested by the above cartoon.

*Print answer here*

# JUMBLE®

Unscramble these four Jumbles, one letter to each square, to form four ordinary words.

ORPEN

NOVEY

RUSHOC

INDARC

WHAT KIDS GET A BIG BANG OUT OF.

Now arrange the circled letters to form the surprise answer, as suggested by the above cartoon.

*Print answer here* THE

20

# JUMBLE®

Unscramble these four Jumbles, one letter to each square, to form four ordinary words.

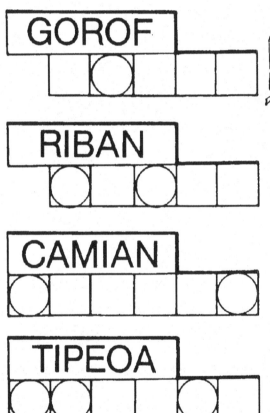

GOROF

RIBAN

CAMIAN

TIPEOA

WHERE DID THE OLD LADY WHO LIVED IN A SHOE SEND HER KIDS WHEN THEY GREW UP?

Now arrange the circled letters to form the surprise answer, as suggested by the above cartoon.

*Print answer here* TO " ⬡⬡⬡⬡ " ⬡⬡⬡⬡

# JUMBLE®

Unscramble these four Jumbles, one letter to
each square, to form four ordinary words.

ROPEA

DUGEN

TAJUNY

GLYFAD

WHAT DRACULA PO-
LITELY SAID, AFTER
ENJOYING HIS USUAL
GUSTATORY TREATS.

Now arrange the circled letters to form the
surprise answer, as suggested by the above
cartoon.

*Print answer here* "  "

# JUMBLE®

Unscramble these four Jumbles, one letter to
each square, to form four ordinary words.

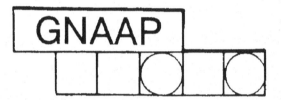

GNAAP

SEHCS

DANGIE

YUIRPT

I think she misunderstood

SHE SAID SHE WAS
EXPECTING TO BECOME
ENGAGED, BECAUSE HER
BOYFRIEND TOLD HER
HE'D GIVE HER THIS.

Now arrange the circled letters to form the
surprise answer, as suggested by the above
cartoon.

*Print answer here* A  ONE

23

# JUMBLE®

Unscramble these four Jumbles, one letter to
each square, to form four ordinary words.

ELZAH

LAWRD

CROFIL

TEFNIC

See? I told you so

WHAT WAS THE STORY
ABOUT THE DOG THAT
CHASED THE STICK
FOR TWO MILES?

Now arrange the circled letters to form the
surprise answer, as suggested by the above
cartoon.

*Print answer here* "⬜⬜⬜ ⬜⬜⬜⬜⬜⬜⬜⬜"

# JUMBLE®

Unscramble these four Jumbles, one letter to each square, to form four ordinary words.

KEVOE

TUMON

SWEENT

UFTOIT

WHAT KIND OF MUSIC DID THE FIDDLER'S SQUEAKING SHOES MAKE?

Now arrange the circled letters to form the surprise answer, as suggested by the above cartoon.

*Print answer here* " ⬡⬡⬡⬡ ⬡⬡⬡⬡⬡ "

# JUMBLE®

Unscramble these four Jumbles, one letter to each square, to form four ordinary words.

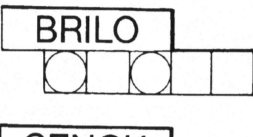

**BRILO**

**CENOU**

**MEBBUN**

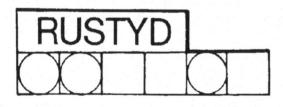

**RUSTYD**

THE KANGAROO PROVED TO BE A VALUABLE MEMBER OF THE FOOT-BALL TEAM BECAUSE HE WAS NEVER THIS.

Now arrange the circled letters to form the surprise answer, as suggested by the above cartoon.

*Print answer here*   OF

# JUMBLE®

Unscramble these four Jumbles, one letter to each square, to form four ordinary words.

HARAJ

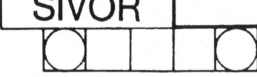

SIVOR

KLANTE

GODINI

PROVIDES THE MAIN COURSE ON A FLIGHT.

Now arrange the circled letters to form the surprise answer, as suggested by the above cartoon.

*Print answer here* THE

# JUMBLE®

Unscramble these four Jumbles, one letter to
each square, to form four ordinary words.

FRADT

EAPEY

LUFOWE

DARCCO

THE SWIMMING POOL
WAS MORE THAN
HE COULD AFFORD,
AND NOW HE'S---

Now arrange the circled letters to form the
surprise answer, as suggested by the above
cartoon.

*Print answer here* IN ☐☐☐☐☐ ☐☐☐☐☐

# JUMBLE®

Unscramble these four Jumbles, one letter to
each square, to form four ordinary words.

**BROEP**

**VELED**

**INJOAD**

**TUMONT**

Whew! That does it

SHE'LL NO LONGER
STAND FOR BEING
PAINTED.

Now arrange the circled letters to form the
surprise answer, as suggested by the above
cartoon.

*Print answer here* A

# JUMBLE®

Unscramble these four Jumbles, one letter to each square, to form four ordinary words.

LOUFT

DULEE

SORABB

PAWNEO

Health Club

THE BEST PLACE TO KEEP YOUR WEIGHT DOWN.

Now arrange the circled letters to form the surprise answer, as suggested by the above cartoon.

*Print answer here* ◯◯◯◯◯ THE ◯◯◯◯

# JUMBLE®

Unscramble these four Jumbles, one letter to each square, to form four ordinary words.

TAGUM

KELLN

NECTED

ENLOUG

WHAT WORD FORMED IN HIS MIND FROM CONTEMPLATING THAT "NEAT LEG"?

Now arrange the circled letters to form the surprise answer, as suggested by the above cartoon.

**Print answer here** "  "

# JUMBLE®

Unscramble these four Jumbles, one letter to
each square, to form four ordinary words.

**KAHIK**

**GORPY**

**YOJECK**

**DAWTOR**

WHAT KIDS NEVER
PLAY IN SCHOOL.

Now arrange the circled letters to form the
surprise answer, as suggested by the above
cartoon.

*Print answer here*

# JUMBLE®

Unscramble these four Jumbles, one letter to
each square, to form four ordinary words.

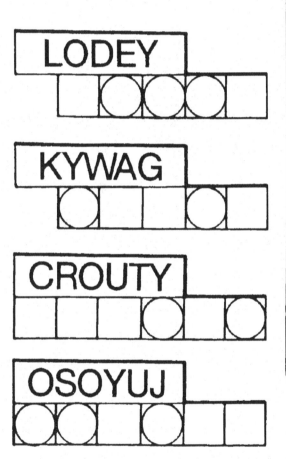

LODEY

KYWAG

CROUTY

OSOYUJ

PUT THIS ON
A HORSE THAT'S
EXPECTED TO WIN.

Now arrange the circled letters to form the
surprise answer, as suggested by the above
cartoon.

*Print answer here* A ⬚⬚⬚⬚ ⬚⬚⬚⬚⬚⬚

# JUMBLE®

Unscramble these four Jumbles, one letter to each square, to form four ordinary words.

**BOVAR**

**YUNTT**

**REGEME**

**GRUHNY**

HE MADE EVERY MINUTE COUNT WHICH IS WHY THEY CALLED HIM THIS.

Now arrange the circled letters to form the surprise answer, as suggested by the above cartoon.

*Print answer here* " ☐☐☐ OF THE ☐☐☐☐ "

# JUMBLE®

Unscramble these four Jumbles, one letter to
each square, to form four ordinary words.

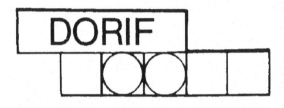

DORIF

PENTI

MORNED

ENMURB

WHEN THE SHIP IS
IN THE HARBOR, THE
MEN IN PORT
MIGHT BE THIS.

Now arrange the circled letters to form the
surprise answer, as suggested by the above
cartoon.

*Print answer here* "  "

# JUMBLE®

Unscramble these four Jumbles, one letter to
each square, to form four ordinary words.

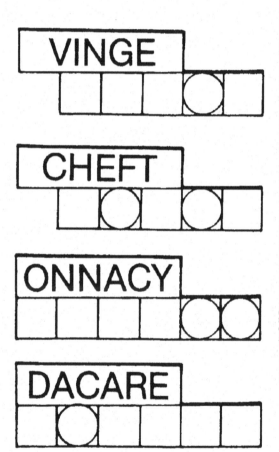

VINGE

CHEFT

ONNACY

DACARE

Place has
changed since I
was last here

PIZZA

BURG

AGAIN IN PARIS!

Now arrange the circled letters to form the
surprise answer, as suggested by the above
cartoon.

**Print answer here** "  "

# JUMBLE®

Unscramble these four Jumbles, one letter to
each square, to form four ordinary words.

**RIDUL**

**YORIN**

**LENKEN**

**WELDIM**

WHAT A FACE
DRAWN WITH CARE
MIGHT BE.

Now arrange the circled letters to form the
surprise answer, as suggested by the above
cartoon.

**Print answer here**

# JUMBLE®

Unscramble these four Jumbles, one letter to
each square, to form four ordinary words.

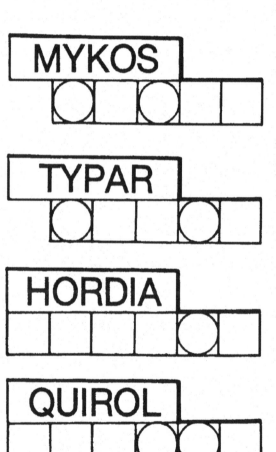

**MYKOS**

**TYPAR**

**HORDIA**

**QUIROL**

WHAT HE DID WHEN
THE DOCTOR SUG-
GESTED HE TRY SOME
WEIGHT LIFTING.

Now arrange the circled letters to form the
surprise answer, as suggested by the above
cartoon.

**Print answer here**

Unscramble these four Jumbles, one letter to
each square, to form four ordinary words.

**SNUKK**

**JYTET**

**BUESAD**

**CRAHNB**

Ugh!

BACK IN THE NAVY.

Now arrange the circled letters to form the
surprise answer, as suggested by the above
cartoon.

*Print answer here*

# JUMBLE.

Unscramble these four Jumbles, one letter to
each square, to form four ordinary words.

GUNTS

EMYTH

ANNOYE

MOINCE

WHY NOT JOIN US
IF YOU'VE---

SUNLOVERS CLUB

Now arrange the circled letters to form the
surprise answer, as suggested by the above
cartoon.

**Print answer here**

# JUMBLE®

Unscramble these four Jumbles, one letter to
each square, to form four ordinary words.

**RANGL**

**ORMUF**

**CECHIT**

**GREBID**

Wrap 'em up!

Wow!

HANDS OUT MONEY
"RIGHT AND LEFT,"
BUT DOESN'T KNOW
HOW TO SPEND IT---

Now arrange the circled letters to form the
surprise answer, as suggested by the above
cartoon.

*Print answer here*

41

# JUMBLE®

Unscramble these four Jumbles, one letter to
each square, to form four ordinary words.

**CLECY**

**DUFIL**

**EXDULP**

**YIELDE**

WHAT YOU MIGHT
DO WHEN YOU NO
LONGER WANT
YOUR BIKE.

Now arrange the circled letters to form the
surprise answer, as suggested by the above
cartoon.

*Print answer here* "  " IT

# JUMBLE®

Unscramble these four Jumbles, one letter to
each square, to form four ordinary words.

GINIC

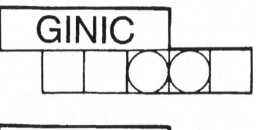

ANAFU

UNTEAR

TOARRO

A MONOGAMIST
DOESN'T BELIEVE IN
BELONGING TO MORE
THAN THIS.

Now arrange the circled letters to form the
surprise answer, as suggested by the above
cartoon.

**Print answer here**

# JUMBLE®

Unscramble these four Jumbles, one letter to each square, to form four ordinary words.

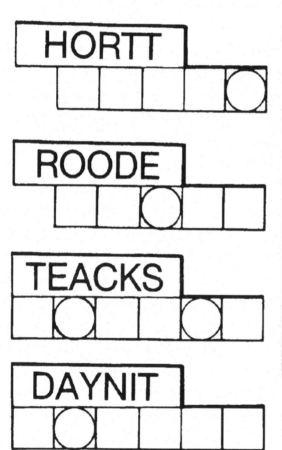

HORTT

ROODE

TEACKS

DAYNIT

STUDENT DRIVER

WHAT YOU HAVE TO FACE IF YOU EXPECT TO LEARN HOW TO DRIVE SAFELY.

Now arrange the circled letters to form the surprise answer, as suggested by the above cartoon.

*Print answer here*

# JUMBLE®

Unscramble these four Jumbles, one letter to each square, to form four ordinary words.

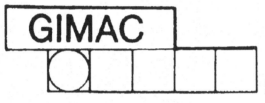

GIMAC

BLYUL

TIBBEG

KOPHOU

I thought you knew what I wanted for breakfast

WHAT TO DO IF YOU DON'T LIKE GRANULATED SUGAR IN YOUR COFFEE.

Now arrange the circled letters to form the surprise answer, as suggested by the above cartoon.

**Print answer here**

# JUMBLE®

Unscramble these four Jumbles, one letter to each square, to form four ordinary words.

LYSHY

GOBEF

SLATTE

RUPPLE

WHAT JOKES TOLD BY AN ABDOMINAL SURGEON ARE APT TO BE.

Now arrange the circled letters to form the surprise answer, as suggested by the above cartoon.

*Print answer here*

# JUMBLE®

Unscramble these four Jumbles, one letter to each square, to form four ordinary words.

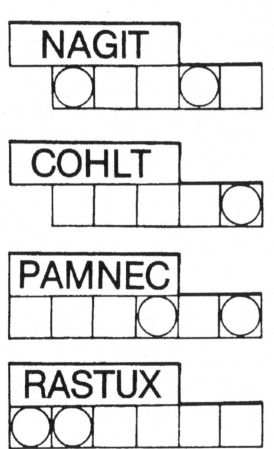

NAGIT

COHLT

PAMNEC

RASTUX

THE ARTIST WENT TO THE PICTURE FRAME SHOP BECAUSE HE HAD SO MANY OF THESE.

Now arrange the circled letters to form the surprise answer, as suggested by the above cartoon.

**Print answer here**

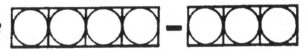

# JUMBLE®

Unscramble these four Jumbles, one letter to each square, to form four ordinary words.

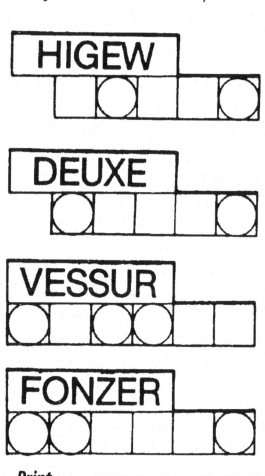

HIGEW

DEUXE

VESSUR

FONZER

WHY SHE LIKED THE GUY WHO ALWAYS BROUGHT STALE BREAD.

Now arrange the circled letters to form the surprise answer, as suggested by the above cartoon.

Print answer here   HE ⬡⬡⬡⬡⬡ GOT " ⬡⬡⬡⬡⬡ "

# JUMBLE®

Unscramble these four Jumbles, one letter to each square, to form four ordinary words.

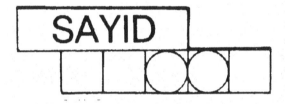

SAYID

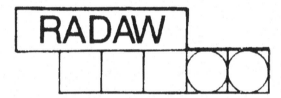

RADAW

THIRDE

BEFLAD

WHICH SIDE OF THE FIRE IS THE HOTTEST?

Now arrange the circled letters to form the surprise answer, as suggested by the above cartoon.

*Print answer here* THE "  "

# JUMBLE®

Unscramble these four Jumbles, one letter to
each square, to form four ordinary words.

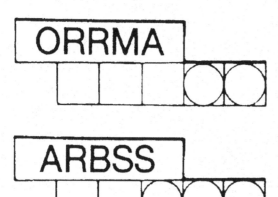

ORRMA

ARBSS

TENAGE

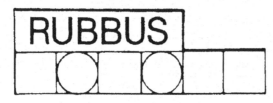

RUBBUS

WHAT A BACKSEAT
DRIVER NEVER DOES,
UNFORTUNATELY.

Now arrange the circled letters to form the
surprise answer, as suggested by the above
cartoon.

Print
answer
here ⬚⬚⬚⬚ ⬚⬚⬚ OF " ⬚⬚⬚ "

Unscramble these four Jumbles, one letter to each square, to form four ordinary words.

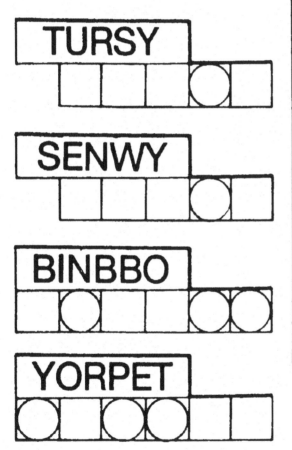

**TURSY**

**SENWY**

**BINBBO**

**YORPET**

HIS SANDWICH ARRIVED SQUASHED BECAUSE HE TOLD THE WAITER TO DO THIS.

Now arrange the circled letters to form the surprise answer, as suggested by the above cartoon.

Print answer here "◯◯◯◯◯ ◯◯ ◯◯"

# JUMBLE®

Unscramble these four Jumbles, one letter to
each square, to form four ordinary words.

**WHASA**

**UNYTT**

**INDIGH**

**LEMITY**

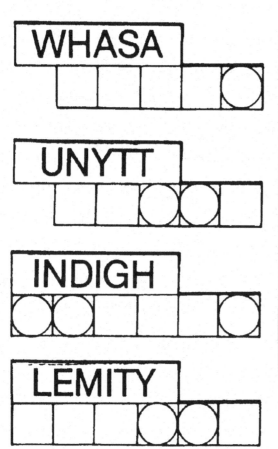

Here
it
is

WHAT'S THE FIRST
THING YOU SEE AFTER
LOOKING FOR SOME-
THING IN THE DARK?

Now arrange the circled letters to form the
surprise answer, as suggested by the above
cartoon.

*Print answer here*

# JUMBLE®

Unscramble these four Jumbles, one letter to
each square, to form four ordinary words.

JONEY

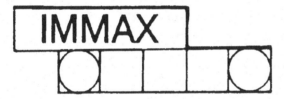

IMMAX

RUBBGY

UMSOQE

My client takes the Fifth

WHAT THEY CALLED
THAT BIG SILENT
ELEPHANT.

Now arrange the circled letters to form the
surprise answer, as suggested by the above
cartoon.

Print
answer A "◯◯◯ - ◯◯ ◯◯◯◯◯◯"
here

# JUMBLE®

Unscramble these four Jumbles, one letter to each square, to form four ordinary words.

UNDOP

EIDUG

DYFLON

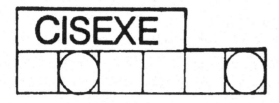
CISEXE

WHAT HE DID
WHEN HE GOT THAT
BIG GAS BILL.

Now arrange the circled letters to form the surprise answer, as suggested by the above cartoon.

**Print answer here**

# JUMBLE®

Unscramble these four Jumbles, one letter to
each square, to form four ordinary words.

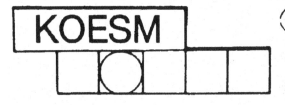

**KOESM**

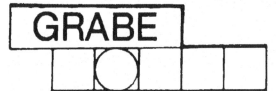

**GRABE**

**YATAPH**

**INFFUM**

WHAT THE
FRUSTRATED ACTOR
TURNED BUTCHER
KNEW HOW TO DO.

Now arrange the circled letters to form the
surprise answer, as suggested by the above
cartoon.

*Print answer here*

# JUMBLE®

Unscramble these four Jumbles, one letter to
each square, to form four ordinary words.

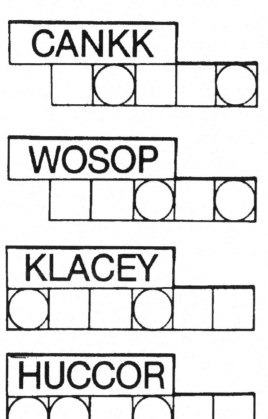

CANKK

WOSOP

KLACEY

HUCCOR

WHAT KIND OF MUSIC
DO YOU GET WHEN
YOU THROW A STONE
INTO THE WATER?

Now arrange the circled letters to form the
surprise answer, as suggested by the above
cartoon.

*Print answer here* " ⟨◯◯◯◯◯⟩ " ⟨◯◯◯◯⟩

# JUMBLE®

Unscramble these four Jumbles, one letter to each square, to form four ordinary words.

OXPRY

FEYHT

DABALL

SUNGUF

WHAT SHE SAID WHEN HER REJECTED SUITOR THREATENED TO JUMP OFF THE CLIFF.

Now arrange the circled letters to form the surprise answer, as suggested by the above cartoon.

**Print answer here** THAT'S ☐☐☐☐☐ A " ☐☐☐☐☐☐ "

# JUMBLE®

Unscramble these four Jumbles, one letter to
each square, to form four ordinary words.

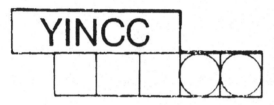

YINCC

NAIGG

SHEERA

CHINTS

HE HAD NO PROBLEM
KEEPING UP HIS END
OF THE CONVERSATION,
BUT A LOT OF
TROUBLE DOING THIS.

Now arrange the circled letters to form the
surprise answer, as suggested by the above
cartoon.

*Print answer here*

# JUMBLE®

Unscramble these four Jumbles, one letter to each square, to form four ordinary words.

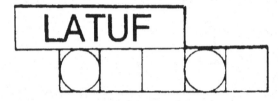

LATUF

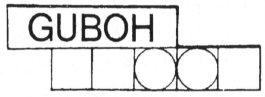

GUBOH

CAFFEE

THOGTE

YOU'LL NEVER LOSE WEIGHT IF YOU TRY TO DO NO MORE THAN THIS.

Now arrange the circled letters to form the surprise answer, as suggested by the above cartoon.

**Print answer here**  IT

# JUMBLE®

Unscramble these four Jumbles, one letter to each square, to form four ordinary words.

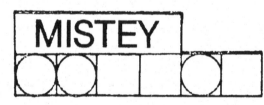

BLAWR

VETEN

ULSSET

MISTEY

Amazing how you held that pose for hours

WITH THIS KIND OF WORK, THE MODEL NEVER SEEMED TO FEEL FATIGUE.

Now arrange the circled letters to form the surprise answer, as suggested by the above cartoon.

*Print answer here* " ⬚⬚ - ⬚⬚⬚⬚⬚⬚⬚⬚ "

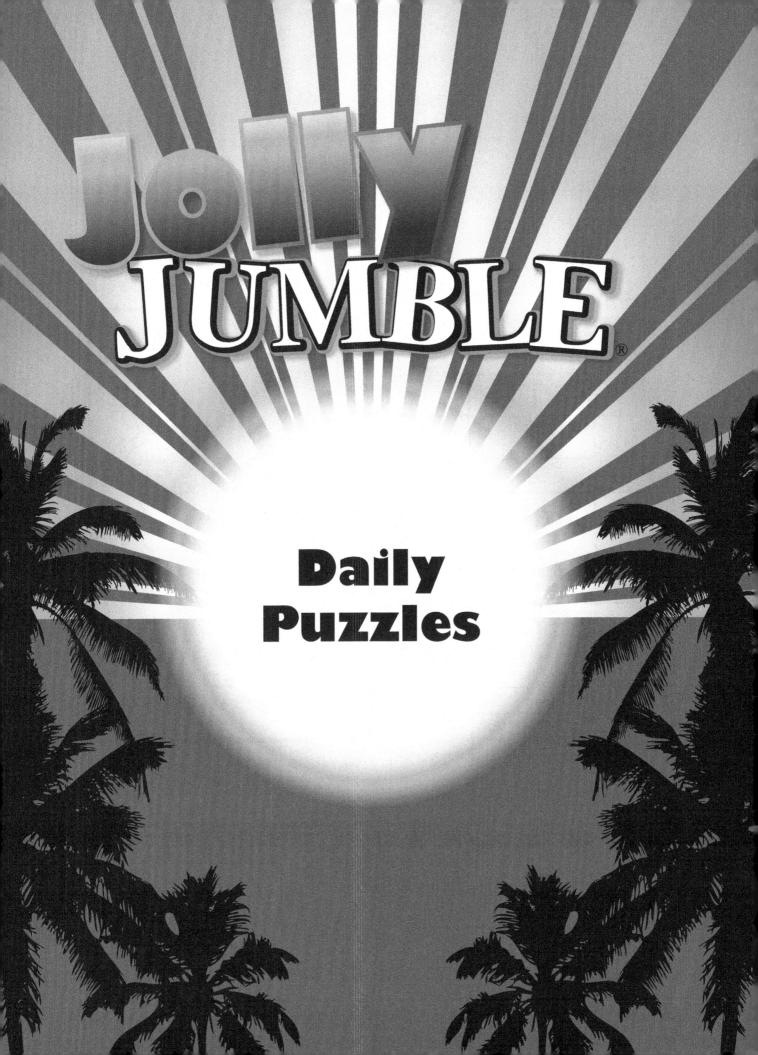

# JUMBLE®

Unscramble these four Jumbles, one letter to
each square, to form four ordinary words.

GUYLB

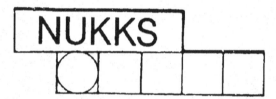

NUKKS

WEEYAL

SOUREA

WHAT THE
CARPENTER WHO
MISPLACED HIS
TOOLS WAS.

Now arrange the circled letters to form the
surprise answer, as suggested by the above
cartoon.

*Print answer here* A " ⃝⃝⃝ " ⃝⃝⃝⃝⃝⃝

# JUMBLE®

Unscramble these four Jumbles, one letter to each square, to form four ordinary words.

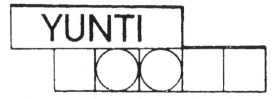

YUNTI

TASUE

CHUNQE

SATECK

SOME PEOPLE GET WHAT THEY WANT BECAUSE THEY HAVE THIS.

Now arrange the circled letters to form the surprise answer, as suggested by the above cartoon.

**Print answer here**  THE " ⭕⭕⭕⭕ – ⭕⭕⭕⭕⭕ "

# JUMBLE®

Unscramble these four Jumbles, one letter to each square, to form four ordinary words.

LITTE

OCKAL

NICKES

TIFFUL

Congratulations! You are a black belt

WHAT HE GOT
WHEN HE TOOK
KARATE LESSONS.

Now arrange the circled letters to form the surprise answer, as suggested by the above cartoon.

 **Print answer here** A ☐☐☐☐☐ ☐☐☐ OF ☐☐

# JUMBLE®

Unscramble these four Jumbles, one letter to
each square, to form four ordinary words.

**VEREF**

**CANET**

**NIFTEC**

**TRALEY**

WHY THEY AVOIDED
THE LATEST
DIET FAD.

Now arrange the circled letters to form the
surprise answer, as suggested by the above
cartoon.

*Print*
*answer* **IT WAS**
*here*

# JUMBLE®

Unscramble these four Jumbles, one letter to each square, to form four ordinary words.

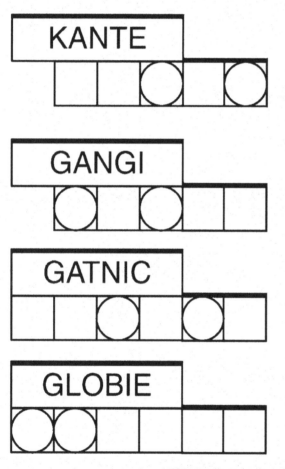

KANTE

GANGI

GATNIC

GLOBIE

Do I get the loan?

You sure do!

WHEN HE APPLIED FOR THE MORT-GAGE, THE LENDER SAID HE COULD----

Now arrange the circled letters to form the surprise answer, as suggested by the above cartoon.

*Print answer here*

# JUMBLE

Unscramble these four Jumbles, one letter to
each square, to form four ordinary words.

RUTYL

RINBY

SIFOSY

TEAZOL

How many cases
have we filled?

AFTER A DAY'S
WORK, THE APPLE
PICKERS SHOWED
THE ---

Now arrange the circled letters to form the
surprise answer, as suggested by the above
cartoon.

*Print
answer
here*

OF THEIR

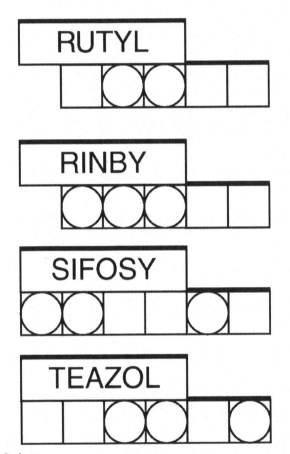

Unscramble these four Jumbles, one letter to each square, to form four ordinary words.

IKYTT

ARSYC

INSOUC

WOINDS

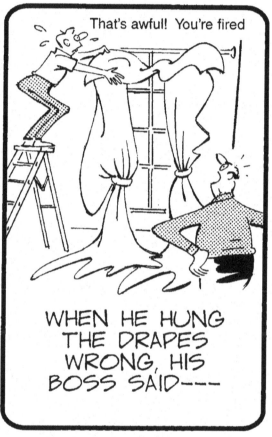

That's awful! You're fired

WHEN HE HUNG
THE DRAPES
WRONG, HIS
BOSS SAID----

Now arrange the circled letters to form the surprise answer, as suggested by the above cartoon.

Print answer here " ☐☐'☐ ☐☐☐☐☐☐☐☐ "

# JUMBLE®

Unscramble these four Jumbles, one letter to each square, to form four ordinary words.

BIMOL

THYIC

MUTTOS

STAFIE

You've been here four times and it still doesn't work

WHAT THE TV REPAIRMAN GOT FROM THE IRATE CUSTOMER.

Now arrange the circled letters to form the surprise answer, as suggested by the above cartoon.

*Print answer here*

 OF " "

# JUMBLE®

Unscramble these four Jumbles, one letter to each square, to form four ordinary words.

BOMUX

LUTEL

GAYPIN

WAIBLE

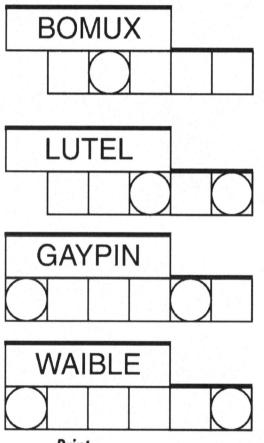

Here comes my curve ball

WHERE THE COW-
BOY PRACTICED
FOR THE BIG
GAME.

Now arrange the circled letters to form the surprise answer, as suggested by the above cartoon.

*Print answer here* **IN THE** " ⬭⬭⬭⬭ ⬭⬭⬭ "

# JUMBLE®

Unscramble these four Jumbles, one letter to each square, to form four ordinary words.

CATHY

GEREM

TINTEK

MEHRIT

No sleep again, Fred?

I feel like a zombie

HOW HE DESCRIBED HIS BOUT WITH INSOMNIA.

Now arrange the circled letters to form the surprise answer, as suggested by the above cartoon.

**Print answer here** A

71

# JUMBLE®

Unscramble these four Jumbles, one letter to
each square, to form four ordinary words.

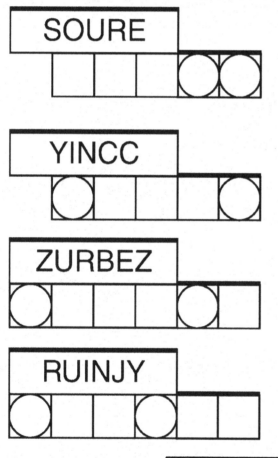

SOURE

YINCC

ZURBEZ

RUINJY

Mom, we're
thirsty again.

FREQUENTLY DROP-
PING IN ON A
HOT DAY.

Now arrange the circled letters to form the
surprise answer, as suggested by the above
cartoon.

 *Print answer here*

72

# JUMBLE®

Unscramble these four Jumbles, one letter to each square, to form four ordinary words.

APANG

BUICC

TRAYPI

HIENAL

She was gorgeous when she was younger

WHAT DO YOU CALL A MODEL TURNED SEAM-STRESS?

Now arrange the circled letters to form the surprise answer, as suggested by the above cartoon.

*Print answer* **A** here

# JUMBLE®

Unscramble these four Jumbles, one letter to each square, to form four ordinary words.

CILLA

GIHLT

WHACES

WHARTT

EASY TO TELL ON HALLOWEEN.

Now arrange the circled letters to form the surprise answer, as suggested by the above cartoon.

*Print answer here* ⬜⬜⬜⬜⬜ IS ⬜⬜⬜⬜⬜

# JUMBLE®

Unscramble these four Jumbles, one letter to
each square, to form four ordinary words.

**TAFEC**

**LEWNY**

**CAFRIB**

**LAGYAX**

Here's twenty to
forget the
whole thing

You've had
it, Buster

WHERE YOU'LL LAND
IF YOU TRY TO
BRIBE A COP.

Now arrange the circled letters to form the
surprise answer, as suggested by the above
cartoon.

*Print
answer
here*  **IN A**  ⬜⬜⬜⬜ " ⬜⬜⬜ "

# JUMBLE.

Unscramble these four Jumbles, one letter to
each square, to form four ordinary words.

GOBUH

FRYOE

SNIULF

HUMBAS

These will make
you well known

WHAT THE YOUNG
ARTIST HOPED FOR
WHEN HE BOUGHT
HIS SUPPLIES.

Now arrange the circled letters to form the
surprise answer, as suggested by the above
cartoon.

Print
answer A "⬡⬡⬡⬡⬡⬡" WITH ⬡⬡⬡⬡
here

# JUMBLE®

Unscramble these four Jumbles, one letter to each square, to form four ordinary words.

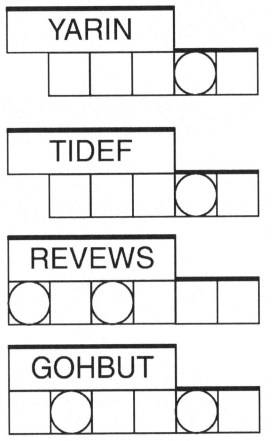

YARIN

TIDEF

REVEWS

GOHBUT

You're right, I'll take all of them

He's a natural!

WHEN THE TRAINEE SOLD HER 5 PAIRS OF HEELS, THE BOSS SAID HE WAS----

Now arrange the circled letters to form the surprise answer, as suggested by the above cartoon.

*Print answer here* **A**

# JUMBLE®

Unscramble these four Jumbles, one letter to
each square, to form four ordinary words.

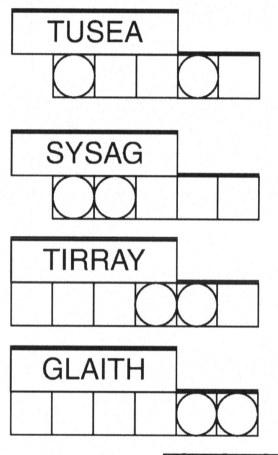

TUSEA

SYSAG

TIRRAY

GLAITH

Here, you drive

WHAT HE DID
WHEN HE HAD
ONE TOO MANY.

Now arrange the circled letters to form the
surprise answer, as suggested by the above
cartoon.

*Print answer here*

# JUMBLE®

Unscramble these four Jumbles, one letter to each square, to form four ordinary words.

BITOR

DEWPI

TOPICE

TRARAT

Watch where you're going

How clumsy of me

WHEN THE VACA-TIONER STUMBLED WHILE SIGHT-SEEING, HE SAID IT WAS——

Now arrange the circled letters to form the surprise answer, as suggested by the above cartoon.

**Print answer here** A

# JUMBLE®

Unscramble these four Jumbles, one letter to
each square, to form four ordinary words.

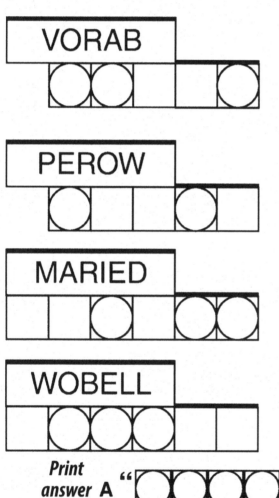

VORAB

PEROW

MARIED

WOBELL

I can't move
the line. Cut it

A SNAG LEFT
THE FISHERMAN
WITH THIS.

Now arrange the circled letters to form the
surprise answer, as suggested by the above
cartoon.

Print
answer **A** " ◯◯◯◯ " ◯◯◯◯◯◯◯
here

Unscramble these four Jumbles, one letter to each square, to form four ordinary words.

ATTIR

YATHS

CAHBLE

LUTTER

...and twenty. Done!

Five, ten...

EASY TO DO WHEN THE SARGE ISN'T LOOKING.

Now arrange the circled letters to form the surprise answer, as suggested by the above cartoon.

*Print answer here* "⬡⬡⬡⬡⬡⬡⬡" **THE** ⬡⬡⬡⬡⬡

# JUMBLE®

Unscramble these four Jumbles, one letter to each square, to form four ordinary words.

VANER

LUGBY

TEACKS

TIPIED

Let's start a protest group

I've been standing in the sun for hours

WHAT THE PAS-
SENGERS FORMED
WHILE WAITING
TO BOARD THE
SHIP.

Now arrange the circled letters to form the surprise answer, as suggested by the above cartoon.

*Print answer here*   A ⬡⬡⬡⬡⬡⬡ " ⬡⬡⬡⬡ "

# JUMBLE®

Unscramble these four Jumbles, one letter to
each square, to form four ordinary words.

ARBSS

NUDET

LEDENE

FOYFAP

8 o'clock, champ.
Time for your
morning run

WHEN THE BOXER
LIKED TO GET
UP.

Now arrange the circled letters to form the
surprise answer, as suggested by the above
cartoon.

Print
answer
here

" "

# JUMBLE

Unscramble these four Jumbles, one letter to
each square, to form four ordinary words.

LIVAL

LOTEX

VESPIL

RECLAN

It's our new
shade and it
lasts all day

Very becoming

WHAT SHE
RECEIVED AT
THE COSMETIC
COUNTER.

Now arrange the circled letters to form the
surprise answer, as suggested by the above
cartoon.

*Print
answer
here*

# JUMBLE®

Unscramble these four Jumbles, one letter to each square, to form four ordinary words.

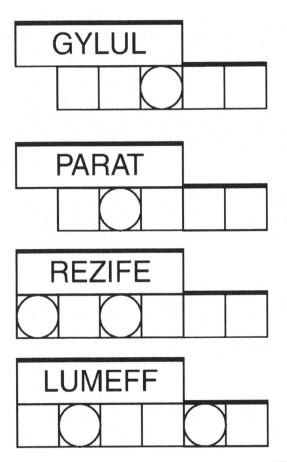

GYLUL

PARAT

REZIFE

LUMEFF

I'm starved

Two candy bars, chips and peanuts

WHY HE STOPPED AT THE GAS STATION.

Now arrange the circled letters to form the surprise answer, as suggested by the above cartoon.

**Print answer here** TO " ⎕⎕⎕⎕ ⎕⎕ "

# JUMBLE®

Unscramble these four Jumbles, one letter to
each square, to form four ordinary words.

CLOON

WILEH

YAWMID

ONSOAL

Steady breathing, and
come up slowly

WHAT THE IN-
STRUCTOR GAVE
THE DIVERS BE-
FORE THEY EN-
TERED THE WATER.

Now arrange the circled letters to form the
surprise answer, as suggested by the above
cartoon.

*Print answer here* **THE** " ⃝⃝⃝⃝⃝⃝⃝ "

# JUMBLE®

Unscramble these four Jumbles, one letter to each square, to form four ordinary words.

UMPEL

KESTO

KEDONY

LUFTAY

Stop pacing. You're making me tired

HOW THE PIANIST FELT BEFORE HIS DEBUT PERFORMANCE.

Now arrange the circled letters to form the surprise answer, as suggested by the above cartoon.

Print answer here

# JUMBLE®

Unscramble these four Jumbles, one letter to each square, to form four ordinary words.

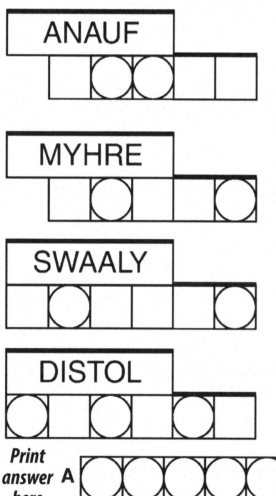

ANAUF

MYHRE

SWAALY

DISTOL

It can sleep eight

We're free next weekend

WHAT THE COUPLE ACQUIRED WHEN THEY BOUGHT A CABIN CRUISER.

Now arrange the circled letters to form the surprise answer, as suggested by the above cartoon.

Print answer here   A ⬭⬭⬭⬭⬭ FOR " ⬭⬭⬭⬭ "

# JUMBLE®

Unscramble these four Jumbles, one letter to each square, to form four ordinary words.

POANC

LIRLT

RIJEGG

SYMICT

We won! We won!

Break out the champagne

WHEN THE PLAYERS WON THE BIG GAME, THEY HAD----

Now arrange the circled letters to form the surprise answer, as suggested by the above cartoon.

*Print answer here*

" "

# JUMBLE®

Unscramble these four Jumbles, one letter to
each square, to form four ordinary words.

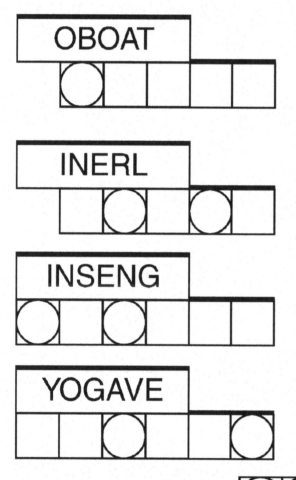

OBOAT

INERL

INSENG

YOGAVE

New lighting...new furniture...

New prices?

THIS IMPROVED
WHEN THE OPTOM-
ETRIST'S OFFICE
WAS REMODELED.

Now arrange the circled letters to form the
surprise answer, as suggested by the above
cartoon.

*Print answer here* **HIS** ⬡⬡⬡ ⬡⬡⬡⬡

# JUMBLE®

Unscramble these four Jumbles, one letter to
each square, to form four ordinary words.

ETHIL

AGGYB

NIGLAC

WEGNIT

I've heard this
song four times

EXPERIENCED BY
MOST WHEN PUT
ON HOLD.

Now arrange the circled letters to form the
surprise answer, as suggested by the above
cartoon.

**Print
answer
here**

◯◯◯◯, ◯◯◯◯◯◯◯

# JUMBLE®

Unscramble these four Jumbles, one letter to each square, to form four ordinary words.

**ZAREC**

**YAHIR**

**GABNIK**

**MOODDE**

Twenty one.
You lose

He's tough
to beat

WHAT THE DEALER ON THE GAMBLING BOAT WAS KNOWN AS.

Now arrange the circled letters to form the surprise answer, as suggested by the above cartoon.

*Print answer here* **A**

# JUMBLE®

Unscramble these four Jumbles, one letter to
each square, to form four ordinary words.

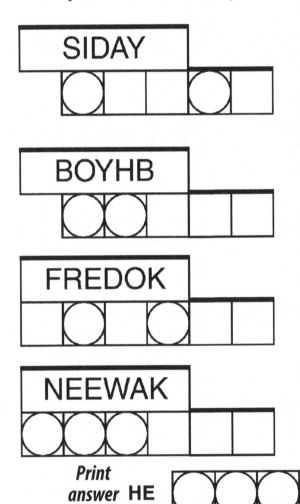

SIDAY

BOYHB

FREDOK

NEEWAK

It's like a
magnet for bass

WHY THE FISHER-
MAN BOUGHT THE
NEW LURE.

Now arrange the circled letters to form the
surprise answer, as suggested by the above
cartoon.

*Print
answer* HE
*here*

# JUMBLE®

Unscramble these four Jumbles, one letter to
each square, to form four ordinary words.

**SIGUE**

**LOGAT**

**NARMOT**

**CUROGH**

The salt and pepper
look is becoming

WHAT SHE SHOWED
WHEN SHE STOPPED
DYEING HER HAIR.

Now arrange the circled letters to form the
surprise answer, as suggested by the above
cartoon.

*Print
answer
here* HER ◯◯◯◯ ◯◯◯◯◯◯

# JUMBLE®

Unscramble these four Jumbles, one letter to each square, to form four ordinary words.

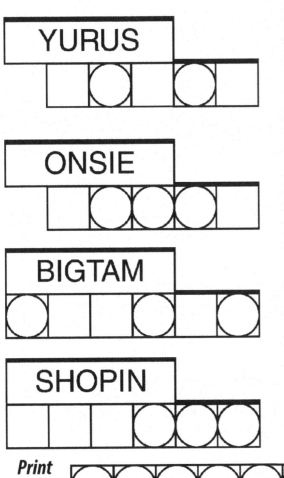

YURUS

ONSIE

BIGTAM

SHOPIN

BRRP...and then we toured the museum...saw all the sights...then we...

HARD TO DIGEST AFTER A BIG MEAL.

Now arrange the circled letters to form the surprise answer, as suggested by the above cartoon.

*Print answer here*

# JUMBLE®

Unscramble these four Jumbles, one letter to
each square, to form four ordinary words.

ORRUJ

LODEY

NINTTE

RUPALL

Leave my kid
brother alone

WHAT THE BULLY
DID WHEN HE
GOT INTO A
"JAM".

Now arrange the circled letters to form the
surprise answer, as suggested by the above
cartoon.

**Print
answer
here**

TO

# JUMBLE®

Unscramble these four Jumbles, one letter to each square, to form four ordinary words.

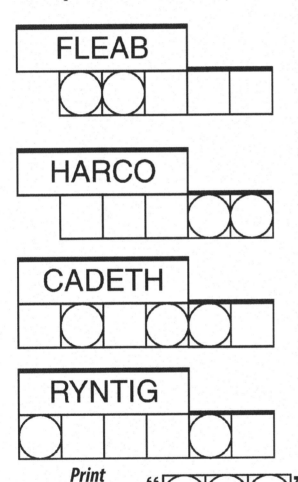

FLEAB

HARCO

CADETH

RYNTIG

Great! That'll REALLY slim you down

WHAT SHE GAVE HER DIETING HUSBAND WHEN HE HAD A MIDNIGHT SNACK.

Now arrange the circled letters to form the surprise answer, as suggested by the above cartoon.

Print answer A here  "◯◯◯" ◯◯◯◯◯◯◯

# JUMBLE®

Unscramble these four Jumbles, one letter to
each square, to form four ordinary words.

CREYM

LAUFT

CEPTID

SCOTUC

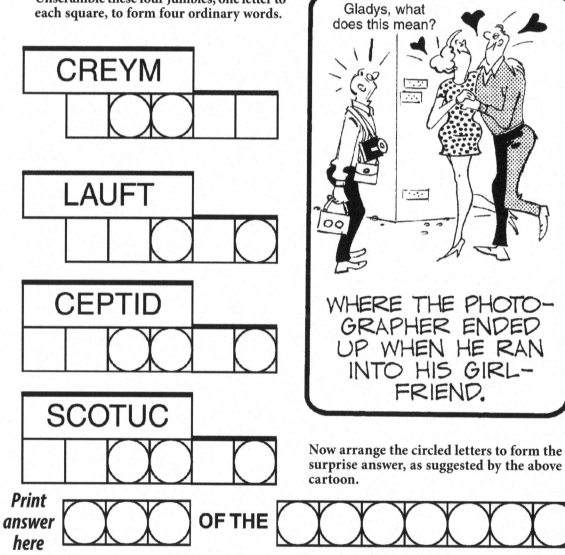

Gladys, what
does this mean?

WHERE THE PHOTO-
GRAPHER ENDED
UP WHEN HE RAN
INTO HIS GIRL-
FRIEND.

Now arrange the circled letters to form the
surprise answer, as suggested by the above
cartoon.

Print
answer
here ⬡⬡⬡ OF THE ⬡⬡⬡⬡⬡⬡⬡

# JUMBLE®

Unscramble these four Jumbles, one letter to each square, to form four ordinary words.

**TENIL**

**RORYS**

**INFEED**

**KADMAS**

WHAT THE COUPLE BECAME WHEN THEY OPENED A SHOE REPAIR SHOP.

Now arrange the circled letters to form the surprise answer, as suggested by the above cartoon.

**Print answer here** " ◯◯◯◯ " ◯◯◯◯◯

# JUMBLE®

Unscramble these four Jumbles, one letter to each square, to form four ordinary words.

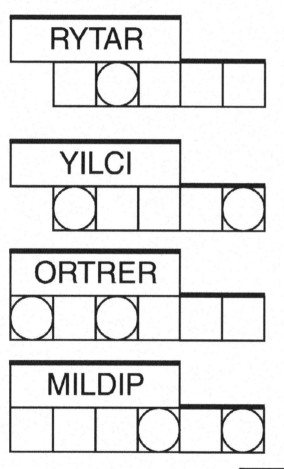

RYTAR

YILCI

ORTRER

MILDIP

It should yield $2000 an acre

A FARMER CAN TURN A FIELD INTO THIS.

Now arrange the circled letters to form the surprise answer, as suggested by the above cartoon.

*Print answer here*

# JUMBLE®

Unscramble these four Jumbles, one letter to
each square, to form four ordinary words.

**SEPOI**

**CHALT**

**BLOUFE**

**AGMANE**

I'm gonna charge
you double

Unless you
want to walk

WHAT THE TOW
TRUCK DRIVER
TRIED TO DO
WHEN THE
SPORTS CAR
BROKE DOWN.

Now arrange the circled letters to form the
surprise answer, as suggested by the above
cartoon.

*Print
answer
here*

 A "   "

# JUMBLE®

Unscramble these four Jumbles, one letter to each square, to form four ordinary words.

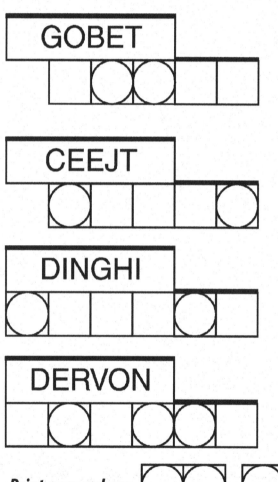

GOBET

CEEJT

DINGHI

DERVON

I love heights

WHERE THE HIGH-RISE RIVETER PREFERRED WORKING.

Now arrange the circled letters to form the surprise answer, as suggested by the above cartoon.

**Print answer here**

# JUMBLE.

Unscramble these four Jumbles, one letter to
each square, to form four ordinary words.

**GLARN**

**TINEW**

**SIDURA**

**LAPEAT**

Remember the
outfits
we wore?

I had a
car like
this in
high school

HOW THEY DROVE
TO THEIR
SCHOOL REUNION.

Now arrange the circled letters to form the
surprise answer, as suggested by the above
cartoon.

*Print
answer
here*  **IN THE** " ⃝⃝⃝⃝ " ⃝⃝⃝⃝

# JUMBLE®

Unscramble these four Jumbles, one letter to
each square, to form four ordinary words.

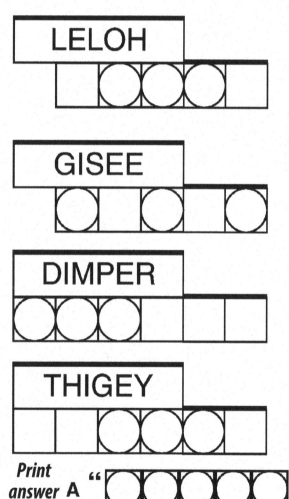

LELOH

GISEE

DIMPER

THIGEY

Leave them
on, please

WHAT JUNIOR
TURNED INTO
AFTER HE SAW
THE MONSTER
MOVIE.

Now arrange the circled letters to form the
surprise answer, as suggested by the above
cartoon.

Print
answer **A**
here

" ☐☐☐☐☐ " ☐☐☐☐☐☐☐

# JUMBLE®

Unscramble these four Jumbles, one letter to
each square, to form four ordinary words.

FATOO

MYMUR

FEEDAC

MAGITS

I'll save money and
lose ten pounds

WHAT SHE DID TO
HER BUDGET
WHEN SHE WENT
ON A DIET.

Now arrange the circled letters to form the
surprise answer, as suggested by the above
cartoon.

*Print
answer
here*

THE

# JUMBLE®

Unscramble these four Jumbles, one letter to
each square, to form four ordinary words.

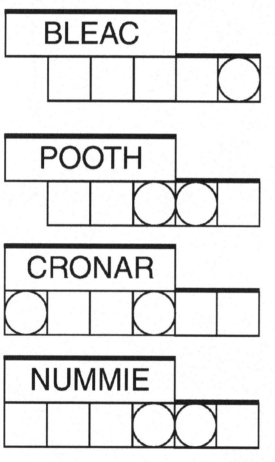

BLEAC

POOTH

CRONAR

NUMMIE

This suit goes on
sale tomorrow

THIS WAS BE—
TWEEN THE SALES-
MAN AND HIS
GOOD CUSTOMER.

Now arrange the circled letters to form the
surprise answer, as suggested by the above
cartoon.

*Print answer here* **THE**

# JUMBLE®

Unscramble these four Jumbles, one letter to
each square, to form four ordinary words.

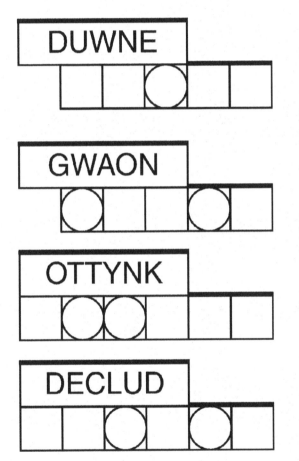

DUWNE

GWAON

OTTYNK

DECLUD

Remember, wheels, flaps, glide path

RECEIVED BY THE
STUDENT PILOT
BEFORE HIS
FIRST LANDING.

Now arrange the circled letters to form the
surprise answer, as suggested by the above
cartoon.

*Print answer here* THE "  "

# JUMBLE®

Unscramble these four Jumbles, one letter to each square, to form four ordinary words.

HETAB

ROJEK

PRAMCE

DIBRYH

Drink plenty of water

WHAT THE SWEATY COWBOY DID ON A HOT DAY.

Now arrange the circled letters to form the surprise answer, as suggested by the above cartoon.

*Print answer here*  "                    "

108

# JUMBLE®

Unscramble these four Jumbles, one letter to each square, to form four ordinary words.

KYMIL

HIRMT

DMAAMN

WEALEY

You're home early

I'll be in the garage

HOW HE FELT WHEN HE WALKED IN ON HIS WIFE'S SEWING CIRCLE.

Now arrange the circled letters to form the surprise answer, as suggested by the above cartoon.

Print answer here " ◯◯◯◯◯◯ " ◯◯

# JUMBLE®

Unscramble these four Jumbles, one letter to each square, to form four ordinary words.

OMBUG

DARTY

RYSHER

SOLUBE

No passes and you'll be swabbing decks for a month

WHAT TIPSY SAILORS FACED WHEN THEY RE- TURNED FROM LEAVE.

Now arrange the circled letters to form the surprise answer, as suggested by the above cartoon.

Print answer here A " ☐☐☐ " OF ☐☐☐☐☐☐☐

# JUMBLE®

Unscramble these four Jumbles, one letter to
each square, to form four ordinary words.

LUDEE

DAMEF

GRIDIF

LUMUTT

You need a smaller size

WHEN THE FOR-
TUNE TELLER
WENT SHOPPING,
THE SALESLADY
SAID SHE WAS----

Now arrange the circled letters to form the
surprise answer, as suggested by the above
cartoon.

*Print answer here* A ⭕⭕⭕⭕⭕⭕

# JUMBLE®

Unscramble these four Jumbles, one letter to each square, to form four ordinary words.

BORIN

HYSIF

VOCENX

NURYGH

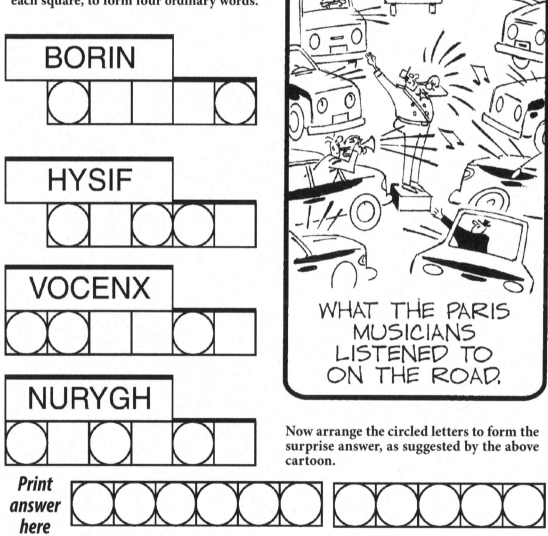

WHAT THE PARIS MUSICIANS LISTENED TO ON THE ROAD.

Now arrange the circled letters to form the surprise answer, as suggested by the above cartoon.

*Print answer here*

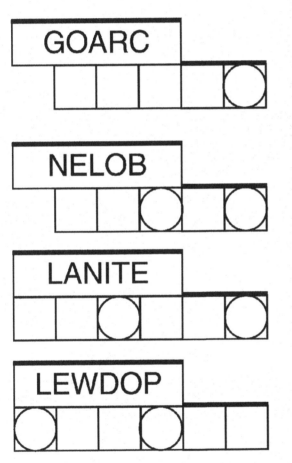

# JUMBLE®

Unscramble these four Jumbles, one letter to
each square, to form four ordinary words.

GOARC

NELOB

LANITE

LEWDOP

Hurry up, I'm late

I'm going as fast
as I can

WHAT THE HAIR-
DRESSER DID
WHEN THE CUS-
TOMER COMPLAINED.

Now arrange the circled letters to form the
surprise answer, as suggested by the above
cartoon.

*Print answer here* ⬭⬭⬭⬭ HER ⬭⬭⬭

113

# JUMBLE®

Unscramble these four Jumbles, one letter to each square, to form four ordinary words.

COHLT

ZISEE

NUGHAT

TORNGS

Nothing fits! I'll starve, go to the fat farm, anything

WHERE SHE WAS WILLING TO GO TO CHANGE HER WIDTH.

Now arrange the circled letters to form the surprise answer, as suggested by the above cartoon.

Print answer TO here

☐☐☐☐☐ "☐☐☐☐☐☐☐"

# JUMBLE®

Unscramble these four Jumbles, one letter to
each square, to form four ordinary words.

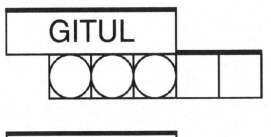

GITUL

RALNS

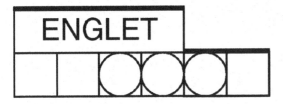

ENGLET

RIPIAM

See? We'll
create a
surreal effect

Charlie, you've
opened my
eyes

WHAT THE DIREC-
TOR CONSIDERED
THE LIGHTING EX-
PERT'S SUGGESTION.

Now arrange the circled letters to form the
surprise answer, as suggested by the above
cartoon.

*Print
answer
here*

# JUMBLE®

Unscramble these four Jumbles, one letter to each square, to form four ordinary words.

WULAF

YOILD

VADCIE

BITTID

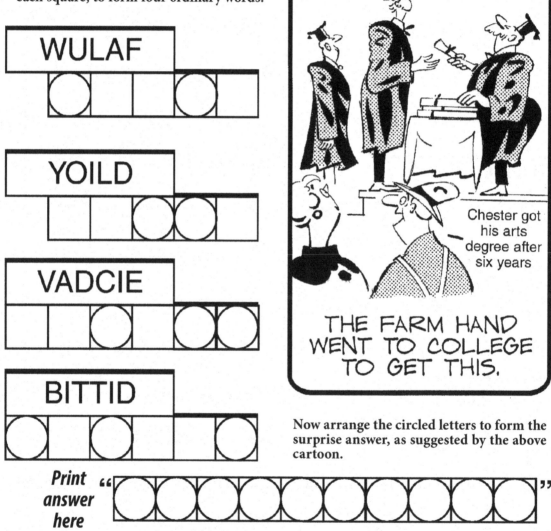

Chester got his arts degree after six years

THE FARM HAND WENT TO COLLEGE TO GET THIS.

Now arrange the circled letters to form the surprise answer, as suggested by the above cartoon.

*Print answer here* " ◯◯◯◯◯◯◯◯◯◯ "

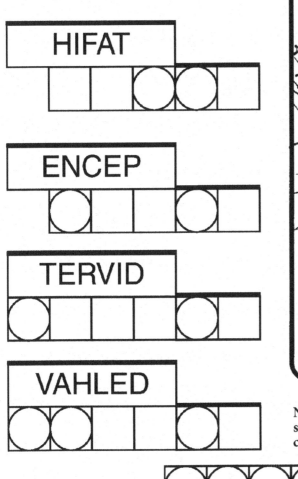

# JUMBLE®

Unscramble these four Jumbles, one letter to each square, to form four ordinary words.

HIFAT

ENCEP

TERVID

VAHLED

FINAL CLEARANCE

They're practically nothing

THE DOWN-TO-EARTH SHOPPER BOUGHT THE DRESSES BECAUSE THEY WERE----

Now arrange the circled letters to form the surprise answer, as suggested by the above cartoon.

Print answer here

# JUMBLE®

Unscramble these four Jumbles, one letter to
each square, to form four ordinary words.

LYJOL

SASEY

DASSIT

INFFUM

I'll cut all taxes

Same
old
baloney

VOTE
FO

JOHN

FOR HONEST JOHN

WHAT THE CANDI-
DATE'S "SOUND"
PLAN TURNED
INTO.

Now arrange the circled letters to form the
surprise answer, as suggested by the above
cartoon.

**Print answer here**

# JUMBLE®

Unscramble these four Jumbles, one letter to
each square, to form four ordinary words.

**EXOID**

**YANDD**

**KLEESH**

**YANTID**

The premium
polish is $50

Worth
every
penny

HOW THE MANI-
CURIST MADE
MONEY.

Now arrange the circled letters to form the
surprise answer, as suggested by the above
cartoon.

*Print answer here* "◯◯◯◯◯ - ◯◯◯"

# JUMBLE®

Unscramble these four Jumbles, one letter to each square, to form four ordinary words.

BIANC

TYIED

INCLEP

MOECEB

I know
the Mayor

Yeah, sure

WHAT THE MOB
BOSS SAID WHEN
HE WAS
ARRESTED.

Now arrange the circled letters to form the surprise answer, as suggested by the above cartoon.

Print
answer
here

" ◯ ' ◯ ◯◯◯◯◯◯◯◯◯ "

# JUMBLE®

Unscramble these four Jumbles, one letter to
each square, to form four ordinary words.

**GUGOE**

**DOREL**

**NESSUC**

**SWEDIT**

Just a few more
things to do

WHAT MOM TIED
UP ON CHRIST-
MAS EVE.

Now arrange the circled letters to form the
surprise answer, as suggested by the above
cartoon.

**Print answer here** ⬡⬡⬡⬡⬡ ⬡⬡⬡⬡

121

# JUMBLE®

Unscramble these four Jumbles, one letter to
each square, to form four ordinary words.

TROFY

VENIA

EXLUDE

GLUCED

There
goes my
business

HOW THE NEW
VENDOR FELT
WHEN HE LOST
THE BALLOONS.

Now arrange the circled letters to form the
surprise answer, as suggested by the above
cartoon.

*Print answer here*

# JUMBLE®

Unscramble these four Jumbles, one letter to
each square, to form four ordinary words.

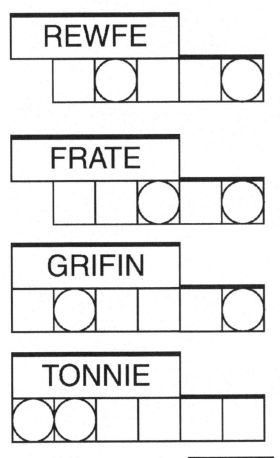

REWFE

FRATE

GRIFIN

TONNIE

So many of
these...enough
is enough

WHAT THE AGING
MECHANIC CON-
SIDERED WHILE
CHANGING THE
BALDING WHEELS.

Now arrange the circled letters to form the
surprise answer, as suggested by the above
cartoon.

*Print answer here* " ◯◯ - ◯◯◯◯◯◯◯ "

# JUMBLE®

Unscramble these four Jumbles, one letter to each square, to form four ordinary words.

BREYD

HOUTY

SWEENT

DOXUTE

Three to one the champ knocks him out

Five to one he loses

WHY THE FRIENDS ARGUED AT THE BOXING MATCH.

Now arrange the circled letters to form the surprise answer, as suggested by the above cartoon.

Print answer here ⬡⬡⬡⬡ ⬡⬡⬡⬡ AT ⬡⬡⬡⬡

Unscramble these four Jumbles, one letter to
each square, to form four ordinary words.

**DYGUP**

**HESEP**

**RIQUMS**

**EPTTIE**

Where'd you
get 'em?

Come
with
us

WHAT THE FANCY
NEW SHOES DID
TO THE VAGRANT.

Now arrange the circled letters to form the
surprise answer, as suggested by the above
cartoon.

*Print
answer
here*

# JUMBLE®

Unscramble these four Jumbles, one letter to each square, to form four ordinary words.

CHITH

SNAPY

RETHOX

SAYQUE

Four are missing

Gee, they were here a minute ago

HOW THE HERDER'S HELPER FELT WHEN HE LOST THE LAMBS.

Now arrange the circled letters to form the surprise answer, as suggested by the above cartoon.

**Print answer here** " ⎣◯◯◯◯◯◯◯◯⎦ "

# JUMBLE®

Unscramble these four Jumbles, one letter to each square, to form four ordinary words.

VEDEL

UDGIE

NALDIN

ROWDYS

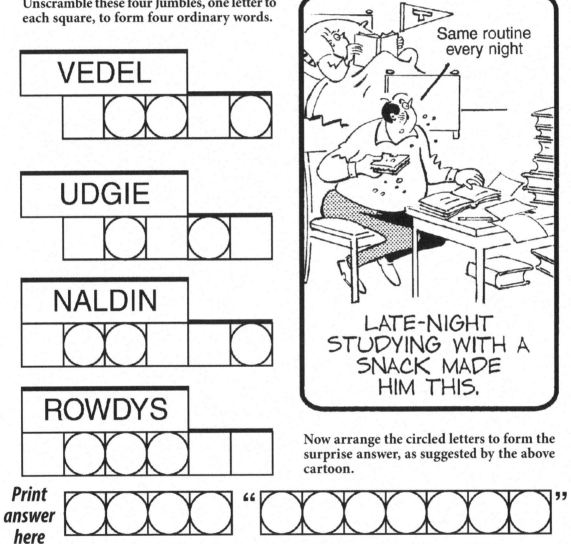

Same routine every night

LATE-NIGHT STUDYING WITH A SNACK MADE HIM THIS.

Now arrange the circled letters to form the surprise answer, as suggested by the above cartoon.

*Print answer here*

"                                    "

127

# JUMBLE®

Unscramble these four Jumbles, one letter to
each square, to form four ordinary words.

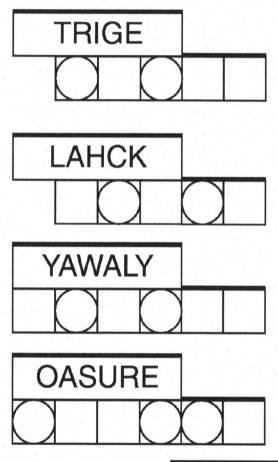

TRIGE

LAHCK

YAWALY

OASURE

WHAT THE CLOWNS
ENDED UP WITH
AT THE CIRCUS
FINALE.

Now arrange the circled letters to form the
surprise answer, as suggested by the above
cartoon.

**Print answer here** THE ⬡⬡⬡⬡ ⬡⬡⬡⬡⬡

# JUMBLE®

Unscramble these four Jumbles, one letter to each square, to form four ordinary words.

**ROBOD**

**WOYLL**

**LAIWHE**

**SHATAM**

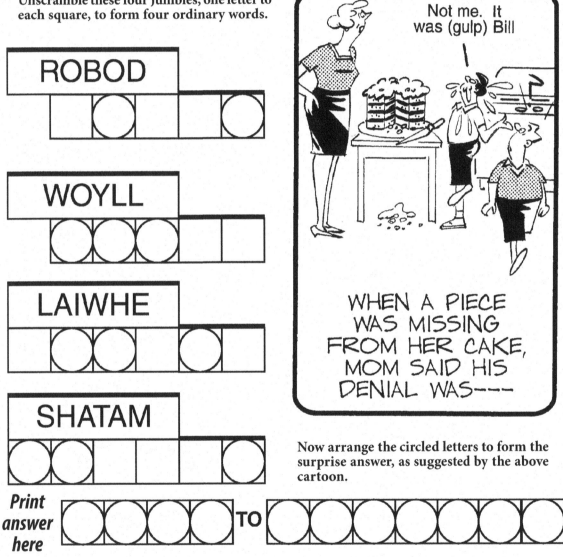

Not me. It was (gulp) Bill

WHEN A PIECE WAS MISSING FROM HER CAKE, MOM SAID HIS DENIAL WAS----

Now arrange the circled letters to form the surprise answer, as suggested by the above cartoon.

**Print answer here**

TO

# JUMBLE®

Unscramble these four Jumbles, one letter to each square, to form four ordinary words.

**SKUDY**

**SPUHL**

**CROITE**

**NIDIOE**

Everything on it

Mmm... hits the spot

WHAT THE BUSY WORKER DID WHEN HE GRABBED A FAST HOT DOG.

Now arrange the circled letters to form the surprise answer, as suggested by the above cartoon.

*Print answer here* **HE** " ◯◯◯◯◯◯◯ " ◯◯

# JUMBLE®

Unscramble these four Jumbles, one letter to
each square, to form four ordinary words.

LONEV

PIRGE

NOBBIB

CLEMUS

We'll
miss you

Let's keep
in touch

SOLD

SAYING GOOD-BYE
TO NEIGHBORS
CAN BE THIS,

Now arrange the circled letters to form the
surprise answer, as suggested by the above
cartoon.

Print
answer
here

A " ◯◯◯◯◯◯ " ◯◯◯◯◯

# JUMBLE®

Unscramble these four Jumbles, one letter to
each square, to form four ordinary words.

**WEHIN**

**PLITO**

**GUNTOE**

**TROBEH**

I hope
she trips

Maybe she'll get
a leg cramp

WHAT THE
DANCERS DID
DURING THE
BALLET TRYOUTS.

Now arrange the circled letters to form the
surprise answer, as suggested by the above
cartoon.

*Print
answer
here*

TO

132

# JUMBLE®

Unscramble these four Jumbles, one letter to
each square, to form four ordinary words.

ELVRO

PLYAP

NEAFED

CLUNKO

Go to your room

WHEN JUNIOR WAS
GROUNDED, HE
LEFT WITH THIS.

Now arrange the circled letters to form the
surprise answer, as suggested by the above
cartoon.

Print
answer
here

A " ◯◯◯◯◯ " ◯◯◯◯

# JUMBLE®

Unscramble these four Jumbles, one letter to
each square, to form four ordinary words.

LUSKK

YOWNS

VALMER

DAPNIK

I can't stand
the daily grind

WHY THE KNIFE
SHARPENER QUIT
HIS JOB.

Now arrange the circled letters to form the
surprise answer, as suggested by the above
cartoon.

Print
answer
here

IT'S " ◯◯◯◯ " ◯◯◯◯

# JUMBLE®

Unscramble these four Jumbles, one letter to
each square, to form four ordinary words.

ADUCT

GUCHO

OCCRAD

LESING

Sam, you look tired.
I'll take over for you

OFTEN DONE BY
A HELPFUL
LATHE OPERATOR.

Now arrange the circled letters to form the
surprise answer, as suggested by the above
cartoon.

*Print answer here* A ◯◯◯◯◯ " ◯◯◯◯ "

# JUMBLE®

Unscramble these four Jumbles, one letter to each square, to form four ordinary words.

**DRIAP**

**RANEY**

**CEITED**

**SLEAWE**

You spent $400?  It goes with all my outfits

WHAT SHE GOT WHEN SHE BOUGHT THAT HANDBAG.

Now arrange the circled letters to form the surprise answer, as suggested by the above cartoon.

*Print answer here*  " ◯◯◯◯◯◯◯ "  ◯◯◯◯

# JUMBLE®

Unscramble these four Jumbles, one letter to each square, to form four ordinary words.

TARFD

WRAFE

CAFFEE

NEWECH

Mmm, these fries are good

So what's new, Harry?

WHAT THE FRIENDS DID WHEN THEY ATE THEIR FAST FOOD LUNCH.

Now arrange the circled letters to form the surprise answer, as suggested by the above cartoon.

*Print answer here*

THE " "

# JUMBLE®

Unscramble these four Jumbles, one letter to
each square, to form four ordinary words.

RUFIT

VOACH

VEENAL

RUHLOY

Honey, all of a
sudden we're rich

WHERE THE BEE-
KEEPER FOUND
HIMSELF WHEN
HIS HONEY SALES
TRIPLED.

Now arrange the circled letters to form the
surprise answer, as suggested by the above
cartoon.

*Print
answer
here*    IN

# JUMBLE®

Unscramble these four Jumbles, one letter to each square, to form four ordinary words.

KLEAY

BAITH

ANGOLO

NUTBOT

It's been 2 years, 4 months, and 5 days

But he chews 3 packs of gum a day

HE COULDN'T STOP THIS WHEN HE QUIT SMOKING.

Now arrange the circled letters to form the surprise answer, as suggested by the above cartoon.

*Print answer here*

IT

# JUMBLE.

Unscramble these four Jumbles, one letter to each square, to form four ordinary words.

YAGIL

BROEP

BLOMIE

ENJUKT

It's so noisy

WHAT THE FIRE-WORKS CREW DID AT THE CELEBRA-TION.

Now arrange the circled letters to form the surprise answer, as suggested by the above cartoon.

Print answer here

A " ⬡⬡⬡⬡⬡ " ⬡⬡ ⬡⬡⬡⬡

140

# JUMBLE®

Unscramble these four Jumbles, one letter to
each square, to form four ordinary words.

**REESA**

**RIDUL**

**NELPOY**

**DULSHO**

He's prompt and efficient

IMPORTANT FOR A
GARBAGE MAN
TO BE.

Now arrange the circled letters to form the
surprise answer, as suggested by the above
cartoon.

**Print
answer AT
here**  " "

# JUMBLE®

Unscramble these four Jumbles, one letter to each square, to form four ordinary words.

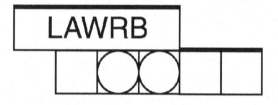

LAWRB

PRUSN

EXDULP

DYGOTS

HOME: 90
VISITORS: 91

That dopey
ref blew
the call

A LOT OF WHINES
COME FROM THIS.

Now arrange the circled letters to form the surprise answer, as suggested by the above cartoon.

**Print
answer
here**

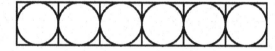

# JUMBLE®

Unscramble these four Jumbles, one letter to
each square, to form four ordinary words.

**MEERY**

**HUBSY**

**TINVER**

**CALHUN**

This must be
the nostalgia
act

THE ORGAN GRINDER
PERFORMED AT THE
STREET FESTIVAL
WHEN IT WAS----

Now arrange the circled letters to form the
surprise answer, as suggested by the above
cartoon.

*Print answer here* ◯◯◯ "◯◯◯◯"

# JUMBLE.

Unscramble these four Jumbles, one letter to each square, to form four ordinary words.

ACOME

FEROC

REDDEG

YURFIP

The sound goes right through you

WHAT HER EARS FELT LIKE AT THE ROCK CONCERT.

Now arrange the circled letters to form the surprise answer, as suggested by the above cartoon.

*Print answer here* " ◯◯◯◯◯◯◯ "

Unscramble these four Jumbles, one letter to
each square, to form four ordinary words.

SIFIN

MYALD

TIENIF

INGOPE

A lot of famous
people are
buried here

WHY THE NOVELIST
VISITED THE
CEMETERY.

Now arrange the circled letters to form the
surprise answer, as suggested by the above
cartoon.

*Print
answer
here* TO ◯◯◯◯ " ◯◯◯◯◯ "

# JUMBLE®

Unscramble these four Jumbles, one letter to
each square, to form four ordinary words.

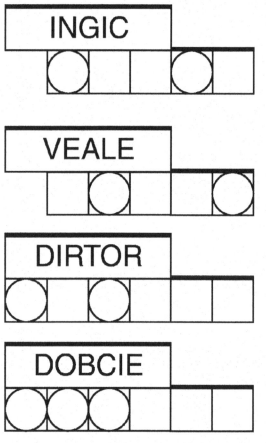

INGIC

VEALE

DIRTOR

DOBCIE

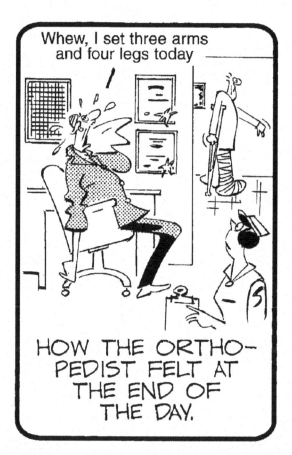

Whew, I set three arms
and four legs today

HOW THE ORTHO-
PEDIST FELT AT
THE END OF
THE DAY.

Now arrange the circled letters to form the
surprise answer, as suggested by the above
cartoon.

Print "⬡⬡⬡⬡" ⬡⬡⬡⬡⬡
answer
here

# JUMBLE®

Unscramble these four Jumbles, one letter to each square, to form four ordinary words.

SOULE

LAAVI

BIUMED

DRAIMY

All he wants to do is crash by the pool

WHAT THE ROCK-STAR BECAME WHEN HE WENT ON VACATION.

Now arrange the circled letters to form the surprise answer, as suggested by the above cartoon.

*Print answer here* AN ◯◯◯◯ ◯◯◯◯

# JUMBLE®

Unscramble these four Jumbles, one letter to each square, to form four ordinary words.

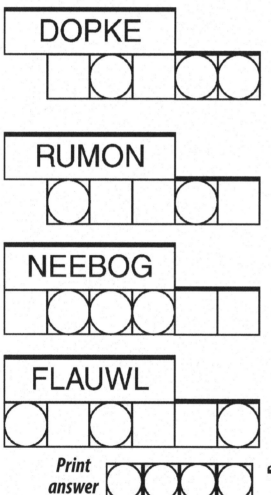

DOPKE

RUMON

NEEBOG

FLAUWL

He's more handsome than ever

HOW HE LOOKED ON HIS WEDDING DAY.

Now arrange the circled letters to form the surprise answer, as suggested by the above cartoon.

*Print answer here*  "        "

# JUMBLE®

Unscramble these four Jumbles, one letter to
each square, to form four ordinary words.

ICHED

MAUHN

BONGLE

VIMOTE

He just cost us three runs

WHEN THE JUDGE
MADE AN ERROR,
HIS TEAMMATES
SAID HE
BELONGED HERE.

Now arrange the circled letters to form the
surprise answer, as suggested by the above
cartoon.

*Print
answer
here*

# JUMBLE®

Unscramble these four Jumbles, one letter to each square, to form four ordinary words.

HUTOM

VERIP

LATOPS

LYRSUT

This is a comedy, role, Peter

I'm laughing already

WHAT THE AVIATOR BECAME WHEN HE AUDITIONED FOR A TV ROLE.

Now arrange the circled letters to form the surprise answer, as suggested by the above cartoon.

Print answer here

A [ ][ ][ ][ ] " [ ][ ][ ][ ][ ][ ] "

# JUMBLE®

Unscramble these four Jumbles, one letter to each square, to form four ordinary words.

RIVOS

YESTT

AHLEEX

KALTEC

The last place I want to be

Nothing but trouble

IRS

THIS AGENT WORKS HERE.

Now arrange the circled letters to form the surprise answer, as suggested by the above cartoon.

Print answer here

A "          "

# JUMBLE®

Unscramble these four Jumbles, one letter to each square, to form four ordinary words.

**OSHUE**

**GUDOH**

**TECTAL**

**INKANP**

Go sit quietly in the corner

Sorry, I won't do it again

WHAT THE CHOIR-BOY DID WHEN HE WAS REPRIMANDED FOR HORSEPLAY.

Now arrange the circled letters to form the surprise answer, as suggested by the above cartoon.

Print answer here

HIS "◯◯◯◯"

# JUMBLE®

Unscramble these four Jumbles, one letter to each square, to form four ordinary words.

KYACT

OSSUE

CLAMIE

GASYRS

Psst, let's sneak out to the ball game

BARBER STUDENTS CAN DO THIS WITH-OUT FEAR OF PENALTY.

Now arrange the circled letters to form the surprise answer, as suggested by the above cartoon.

 *Print answer here*  A

# JUMBLE®

Unscramble these four Jumbles, one letter to each square, to form four ordinary words.

GUNTS

GUNEB

TOCCUL

PHOSUT

It
doesn't
work

It just needs
a few more
adjustments

WHAT DAD DID
WITH HIS NEW
PEST SPRAYER.

Now arrange the circled letters to form the surprise answer, as suggested by the above cartoon.

*Print answer here*  ◯◯◯ THE " ◯◯◯◯◯ " ◯◯◯

# JUMBLE®

Unscramble these four Jumbles, one letter to each square, to form four ordinary words.

INGEF

IRROG

NAPOWE

ICKEOO

The dishes are done. Anything else, dear?

WHEN HE MARRIED FOR MONEY, HE ENDED UP DOING THIS.

Now arrange the circled letters to form the surprise answer, as suggested by the above cartoon.

Print answer here

IT

# JUMBLE®

Unscramble these four Jumbles, one letter to each square, to form four ordinary words.

INNOO

GINOG

HINSIF

LAHMYN

#$%*%!! That's the third shot in the water today

What kind of bait are you using?

WHAT HE ENDED UP DOING WHEN HE WENT GOLFING.

Now arrange the circled letters to form the surprise answer, as suggested by the above cartoon.

*Print answer here*

# JUMBLE®

Unscramble these four Jumbles, one letter to each square, to form four ordinary words.

CELEX

TUCOL

DROLIF

HARTHS

After you, J.B.

CONFERENCE ROOM

Thank you, my boy

THIS CAN LEAD TO NEW OPPORTUNI- TIES IN THE PUSH AND PULL OF BUSINESS.

Now arrange the circled letters to form the surprise answer, as suggested by the above cartoon.

**Print answer here**

157

# JUMBLE®

Unscramble these four Jumbles, one letter to each square, to form four ordinary words.

ALQUI

TUBIL

YASILE

INTOAR

Oh, just what I wanted

Make us a cake

A NEW MIXER CAN CREATE THIS.

Now arrange the circled letters to form the surprise answer, as suggested by the above cartoon.

*Print answer here*

A

158

# JUMBLE®

Unscramble these four Jumbles, one letter to
each square, to form four ordinary words.

PYTEM

YUSHK

SENFUI

LARMIN

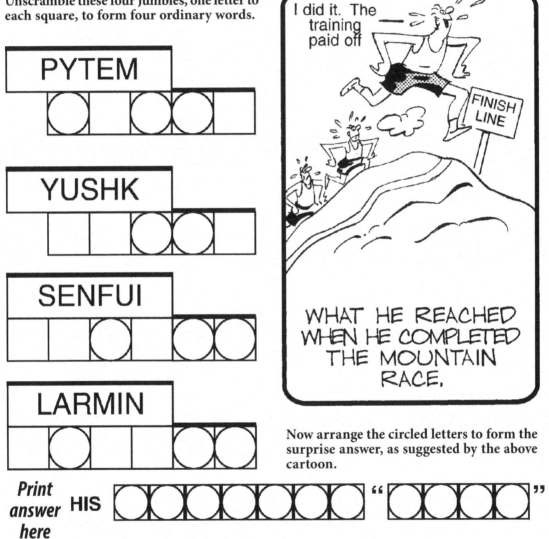

I did it. The _ _ _
training
paid off

FINISH
LINE

WHAT HE REACHED
WHEN HE COMPLETED
THE MOUNTAIN
RACE.

Now arrange the circled letters to form the
surprise answer, as suggested by the above
cartoon.

*Print
answer
here* HIS ⬡⬡⬡⬡⬡⬡ "⬡⬡⬡⬡"

# JUMBLE®

Unscramble these four Jumbles, one letter to
each square, to form four ordinary words.

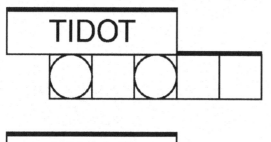

TIDOT

LINAF

GOYNEX

GEENER

TRYOUTS
TODAY

First, I'll make the team,
become a star, and
get drafted

WHEN THE PLAYER
WORKED HARD TO
SUCCEED, HIS
COACH SAID IT
WAS----

Now arrange the circled letters to form the
surprise answer, as suggested by the above
cartoon.

Print
answer
here

# JUMBLE®

Unscramble these four Jumbles, one letter to
each square, to form four ordinary words.

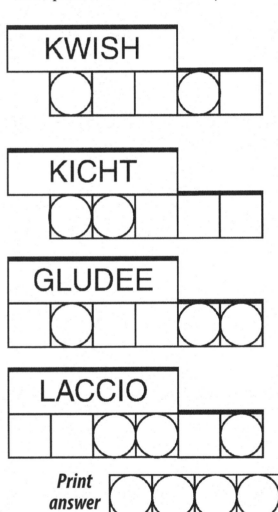

KWISH

KICHT

GLUDEE

LACCIO

Dad, that's your
third helping

WHAT THE LAD
PLANNED TO DO
WHEN HE WAS
BIG AS HIS
FATHER.

Now arrange the circled letters to form the
surprise answer, as suggested by the above
cartoon.

*Print
answer
here*

# JUMBLE®

Unscramble these four Jumbles, one letter to each square, to form four ordinary words.

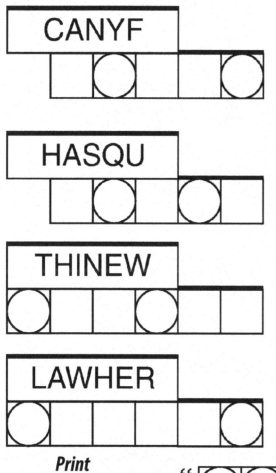

CANYF

HASQU

THINEW

LAWHER

Can't wait to cook 'em

HE WAS DETER-
MINED TO HAVE
SAUSAGES----

Now arrange the circled letters to form the surprise answer, as suggested by the above cartoon.

Print answer here    IN THE "◯◯◯◯◯" ◯◯◯

# JUMBLE®

Unscramble these six Jumbles, one letter to each square, to form six ordinary words.

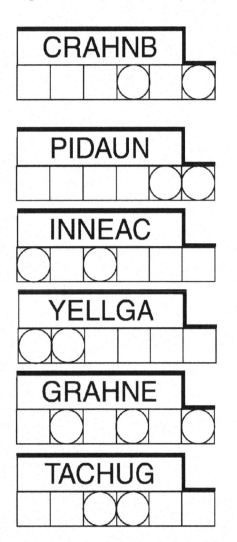

CRAHNB

PIDAUN

INNEAC

YELLGA

GRAHNE

TACHUG

A warm shower and dry clothes

THE RAIN-SOAKED SENTRY LOOKED FORWARD TO THE——

Now arrange the circled letters to form the surprise answer, as suggested by the above cartoon.

*Print answer here*

" ☐☐☐☐☐☐☐☐ " OF THE ☐☐☐☐☐

# JUMBLE®

Unscramble these six Jumbles, one letter to each square, to form six ordinary words.

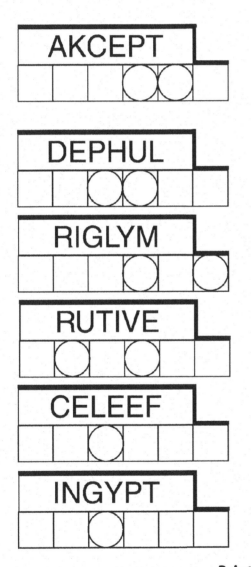

AKCEPT

DEPHUL

RIGLYM

RUTIVE

CELEEF

INGYPT

WHAT BIG SISTER DID WHILE MOM GOT FITTED FOR GLASSES.

Now arrange the circled letters to form the surprise answer, as suggested by the above cartoon.

**Print answer here**

◯◯◯◯ AN ◯◯◯ ON ◯◯◯

165

# JUMBLE

Unscramble these six Jumbles, one letter to
each square, to form six ordinary words.

STIGED

EXCOIB

GROINI

TEPLYN

DUMEGS

RUSTEY

I missed
my friends
here

THE DANCERS RE-
TURNED TO IRELAND
TO GET BACK TO
THEIR OLD----

Now arrange the circled letters to form the
surprise answer, as suggested by the above
cartoon.

*Print answer here*

166

# JUMBLE

Unscramble these six Jumbles, one letter to
each square, to form six ordinary words.

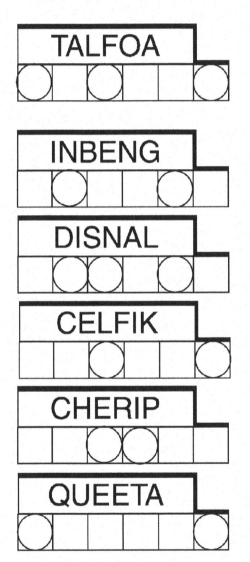

TALFOA

INBENG

DISNAL

CELFIK

CHERIP

QUEETA

Is it
ready?

Hold on,
it takes
longer
up here

MAKING TEA ON A
MOUNTAIN CLIMB
CAN BE A---

Now arrange the circled letters to form the
surprise answer, as suggested by the above
cartoon.

### Print answer here

"◯◯◯◯◯" ◯◯◯◯◯◯◯◯◯

# JUMBLE

Unscramble these six Jumbles, one letter to
each square, to form six ordinary words.

LAUMSY

LANTED

LUCKES

FRIMAF

NERVAG

HELBED

If I win, I'll
be able to
pay my bills

**1ST PRIZE
$1500**

WHY HE ENTERED
THE KNOT-TYING
CONTEST.

Now arrange the circled letters to form the
surprise answer, as suggested by the above
cartoon.

*Print answer here*

TO ⬡⬡⬡⬡ ⬡⬡⬡⬡ ⬡⬡⬡⬡

# JUMBLE®

Unscramble these six Jumbles, one letter to each square, to form six ordinary words.

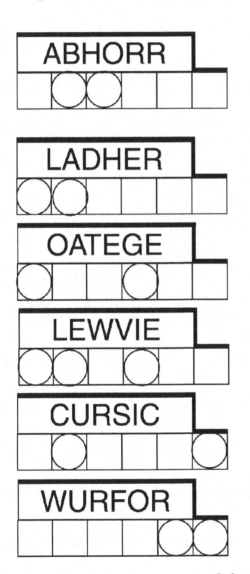

ABHORR

LADHER

OATEGE

LEWVIE

CURSIC

WURFOR

I've got to lose ten pounds in two weeks

You've known about the annual ball for months

WHY SHE DECIDED TO START HER DIET IMMEDIATELY.

Now arrange the circled letters to form the surprise answer, as suggested by the above cartoon.

*Print answer here*

THE ◯◯◯◯◯◯ ◯◯◯ "◯◯◯◯"

# JUMBLE®

Unscramble these six Jumbles, one letter to
each square, to form six ordinary words.

LETHEM

DOGOLY

CONTOY

DACLUN

RITHED

LAFFEB

He has a
booming
practice

Expensive
but worth
it

ENJOYED BY A
SUCCESSFUL
PHYSICIAN.

Now arrange the circled letters to form the
surprise answer, as suggested by the above
cartoon.

*Print answer here*

A "◯◯◯◯◯◯◯" ◯◯◯◯◯◯

# JUMBLE®

Unscramble these six Jumbles, one letter to each square, to form six ordinary words.

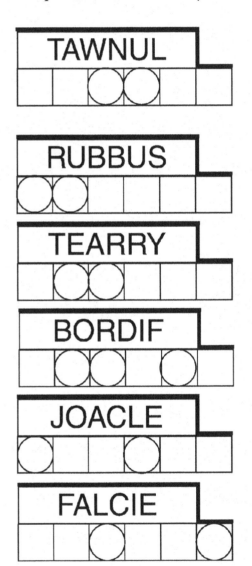

TAWNUL

RUBBUS

TEARRY

BORDIF

JOACLE

FALCIE

Steady as she goes

Aye, aye, sir

NEEDED BY A SHIP'S CAPTAIN ON AN OCEAN VOYAGE.

Now arrange the circled letters to form the surprise answer, as suggested by the above cartoon.

**Print answer here**

171

# JUMBLE®

Unscramble these six Jumbles, one letter to each square, to form six ordinary words.

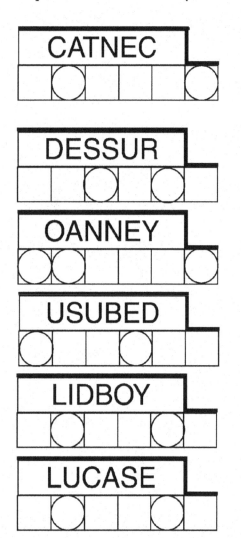

CATNEC

DESSUR

OANNEY

USUBED

LIDBOY

LUCASE

Only $50 an ounce

OFTEN CHANGES HANDS AT A PERFUME COUNTER.

Now arrange the circled letters to form the surprise answer, as suggested by the above cartoon.

*Print answer here*

◯◯◯◯◯◯◯ AND ◯◯◯◯◯◯

Unscramble these six Jumbles, one letter to each square, to form six ordinary words.

CLARGI

GIDINO

NERUNG

MEANIA

YANBOT

NOSTEX

Yes, yes, I did it. I needed it for my lessons

WHAT THE VOICE STUDENT DID WHEN THE BANK WAS ROBBED.

Now arrange the circled letters to form the surprise answer, as suggested by the above cartoon.

**Print answer here**

HE ⬡⬡⬡⬡⬡⬡ "⬡⬡⬡⬡⬡⬡⬡"

# JUMBLE®

Unscramble these six Jumbles, one letter to each square, to form six ordinary words.

BOUTES

YORTHE

RYPTAN

ABNERN

RETAUM

MIRNIF

This #*&% toaster doesn't work!

COMPLAINTS

Sorry, sir — all sales final

WHEN THE BUYER WAS REFUSED A REFUND, HE WAS AT THE---

Now arrange the circled letters to form the surprise answer, as suggested by the above cartoon.

*Print answer here*

⬡⬡⬡⬡⬡⬡ OF "⬡⬡ ⬡⬡⬡⬡⬡⬡"

174

# JUMBLE®

Unscramble these six Jumbles, one letter to
each square, to form six ordinary words.

OILNAB

ALFELN

HUMILS

PUMACS

DAPCIL

RETANB

This is lovely

I wear his outfits

THE WELL-DRESSED
LADIES ATE OFF
DESIGNER DISHES
BECAUSE THEY
WERE---

Now arrange the circled letters to form the
surprise answer, as suggested by the above
cartoon.

*Print answer here*

"◯◯◯◯◯◯◯" ◯◯◯◯◯◯

# JUMBLE®

Unscramble these six Jumbles, one letter to
each square, to form six ordinary words.

HONUKO

LUITED

IMRAUD

LORFIC

CHAPER

DIPSUT

The
silverware
is
tarnished

More
grub,
sir?

THE HOUSEMAID
WAS FIRED BE-
CAUSE SHE----

Now arrange the circled letters to form the
surprise answer, as suggested by the above
cartoon.

*Print answer here*

⎡◯◯◯◯◯◯⎤ " ◯◯◯◯◯◯ "

# JUMBLE®

Unscramble these six Jumbles, one letter to each square, to form six ordinary words.

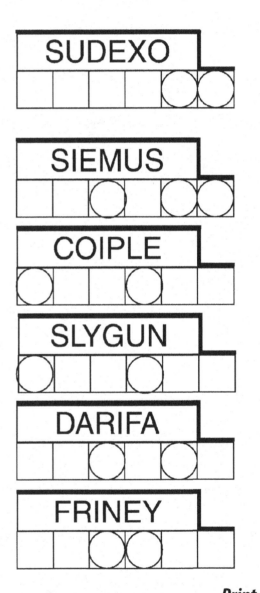

SUDEXO

SIEMUS

COIPLE

SLYGUN

DARIFA

FRINEY

Look! I have to wear this tonight

WHAT THE LAUNDRY FACED WHEN THE SHIRT CAME BACK WRINKLED.

Now arrange the circled letters to form the surprise answer, as suggested by the above cartoon.

*Print answer here*

A " ◯◯◯◯◯◯◯ " ◯◯◯◯◯

# JUMBLE®

Unscramble these six Jumbles, one letter to
each square, to form six ordinary words.

DRAACE

BELFEE

DAMNET

MENIER

REVUPY

MOAPED

But I'm innocent

WANTED

$5000
REWARD

WHAT THE FUGITIVE
SAID WHEN HE SAW
HIS "WANTED"
POSTER.

Now arrange the circled letters to form the
surprise answer, as suggested by the above
cartoon.

*Print answer here*

" ☐ ' ☐☐ ☐☐☐☐☐ ☐☐☐☐☐☐☐ "

# JUMBLE®

Unscramble these six Jumbles, one letter to each square, to form six ordinary words.

SULUFE

SNAFET

ENLOUG

TIPPEC

TEXENT

SNOPER

1% is too low

It's my business and I'll do what I want

WHEN THE BANKER GAVE HIMSELF A LOAN AT A FAVOR- ABLE RATE, IT WAS----

Now arrange the circled letters to form the surprise answer, as suggested by the above cartoon.

## Print answer here

◯◯◯◯ " ◯◯◯◯◯◯◯◯◯ "

# JUMBLE.

Unscramble these six Jumbles, one letter to each square, to form six ordinary words.

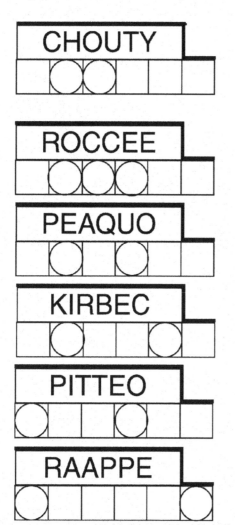

CHOUTY

ROCCEE

PEAQUO

KIRBEC

PITTEO

RAAPPE

$10 to win on Jumble Boy

You got it

USING THE SWITCH-BOARD TO BOOK BETS MADE HIM THIS.

Now arrange the circled letters to form the surprise answer, as suggested by the above cartoon.

*Print answer here*

AN " "

# JUMBLE

Unscramble these six Jumbles, one letter to each square, to form six ordinary words.

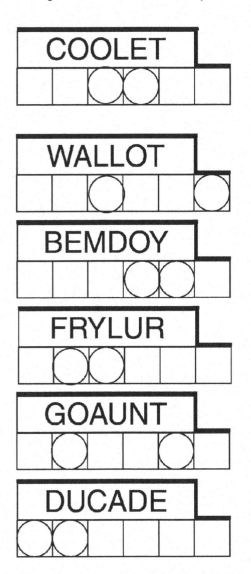

COOLET

WALLOT

BEMDOY

FRYLUR

GOAUNT

DUCADE

WHY THE TEACHER DIDN'T MIND WHEN THE TEST ANSWERS WERE SHOUTED OUT.

Now arrange the circled letters to form the surprise answer, as suggested by the above cartoon.

*Print answer here*

◯◯◯◯◯◯ WAS ◯◯◯◯◯◯◯

# JUMBLE®

Unscramble these six Jumbles, one letter to each square, to form six ordinary words.

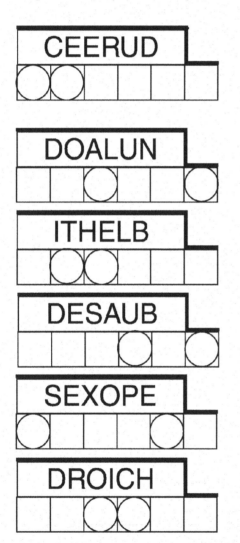

CEERUD

DOALUN

ITHELB

DESAUB

SEXOPE

DROICH

BLOOD GALORE

You must be freezing

TICKETS

But sexy

WHEN SHE WORE
A FLIMSY OUTFIT
ON A COLD NIGHT,
SHE WAS----

Now arrange the circled letters to form the surprise answer, as suggested by the above cartoon.

*Print answer here*  ◯◯◯◯◯◯◯ TO "◯◯◯◯◯"

# JUMBLE®

Unscramble these six Jumbles, one letter to
each square, to form six ordinary words.

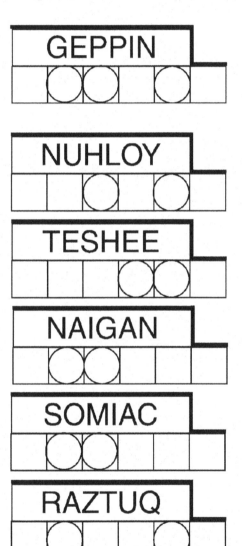

GEPPIN

NUHLOY

TESHEE

NAIGAN

SOMIAC

RAZTUQ

Where's
the
ring,
Bob?

It's
here,
somewhere

WHAT THE NERVOUS
GROOM DIDN'T HAVE ON
HIS WEDDING DAY.

Now arrange the circled letters to form the
surprise answer, as suggested by the above
cartoon.

**Print answer here**

A " ⬡⬡⬡⬡⬡⬡ " ⬡⬡⬡⬡⬡⬡⬡

# Answers

1. **Jumbles:** CROON SNORT MYRIAD ORCHID
**Answer:** What a man sometimes gets from a woman who looks like a dream—INSOMNIA

2. **Jumbles:** GUILD ABHOR KNIGHT BECKON
**Answer:** Back talk is often more honest than this kind of talk—BEHIND-THE-BACK

3. **Jumbles:** RAPID HAREM KINGLY TYCOON
**Answer:** "They're complaining that the lamb is tough"—"LET'S NOT TALK 'CHOP'"

4. **Jumbles:** DOILY VERVE WATERY LARYNX
**Answer:** When a woman "fishes" for a husband she should know this—WHERE TO DRAW THE LINE

5. **Jumbles:** BATCH CHAFF DISOWN IMPORT
**Answer:** Sometimes comes to a head when insults are thrown back and forth—A FIST

6. **Jumbles:** CURRY ABBEY IMPOSE EMBRYO
**Answer:** Went on foot in a rainstorm—RUBBERS

7. **Jumbles:** CROUP FOIST DENTAL WALLOP
**Answer:** Why we woke up feeling down in the mouth—THE PILLOW WAS TORN

8. **Jumbles:** FILMY JADED LOCKET BUBBLE
**Answer:** Might set off an explosion in the home—AN OLD FLAME

9. **Jumbles:** LATHE HITCH GEYSER FRIGID
**Answer:** Sometimes they're a woman's arch enemies—HIGH HEELS

10. **Jumbles:** NERVY CAMEO BEWARE MISHAP
**Answer:** When prices "soar"...—SO ARE WE

11. **Jumbles:** QUOTA TRUTH GRUBBY CEMENT
**Answer:** What the roulette wheel took for a change—A TURN FOR THE "BETTOR"

12. **Jumbles:** JUDGE CHIME EXTENT ADVICE
**Answer:** What happened when four couples when to a restaurant?—EIGHT ATE

13. **Jumbles:** BROIL JUICE EULOGY BAMBOO
**Answer:** What little whales like best—"BLUBBER" GUM

14. **Jumbles:** BROOD MIRTH OUTLAW TRICKY
**Answer:** What they called the hardware store's cat—THE "TOOL KIT"

15. **Jumbles:** BERTH GLORY SWIVEL HOURLY
**Answer:** What the rodeo performer does in order to impress others—THROWS THE BULL

16. **Jumbles:** POISE GRIMY CANINE TORRID
**Answer:** He was so lazy he wouldn't even exercise this—DISCRETION

17. **Jumbles:** REBEL CROON SECEDE TRUANT
**Answer:** When will the mail arrive?—SOONER OR "LETTER"

18. **Jumbles:** CURIO BANDY PREACH MYSELF
**Answer:** What dry-as-dust people never seem to do—DRY UP

19. **Jumbles:** PRONE ENVOY CHORUS RANCID
**Answer:** What kids get a big bang out of—THE DRONES CORE

20. **Jumbles:** FORGO BRAIN MANIAC OPIATE
**Answer:** Where did the old lady who lived in a shoe send her kids when they grew up?—TO "BOOT" CAMP

21. **Jumbles:** OPERA NUDGE JAUNTY GADFLY
**Answer:** What Dracula politely said, after enjoying his usual gustatory treats—"FANG" YOU

22. **Jumbles:** PAGAN CHESS GAINED PURITY
**Answer:** She said she was expecting to become engaged, because her boyfriend told her he'd give her this—A RING ONE NIGHT

23. **Jumbles:** HAZEL DRAWL FROLIC INFECT
**Answer:** What was the story about the dog that chased the stick for two miles?—"FAR FETCHED"

24. **Jumbles:** EVOKE MOUNT NEWEST OUTFIT
**Answer:** What kind of music did the fiddler's squeaking shoes make?—"FOOT NOTES"

25. **Jumbles:** BROIL OUNCE BENUMB STURDY
**Answer:** The kangaroo proved to be a valuable member of the football team because he was never this—OUT OF BOUNDS

26. **Jumbles:** RAJAH VISOR ANKLET INDIGO
**Answer:** Provides the main course on a flight—THE NAVIGATOR

27. **Jumbles:** DRAFT PAYEE WOEFUL ACCORD
**Answer:** The swimming pool was more than he could afford, and now he's—IN DEEP WATER

28. **Jumbles:** PROBE DELVE ADJOIN MUTTON
**Answer:** She'll no longer stand for being painted—A TIRED MODEL

29. **Jumbles:** FLOUT ELUDE ABSORB WEAPON
**Answer:** The best place to keep your weight down—BELOW THE BELT

30. **Jumbles:** GAMUT KNELL DECENT LOUNGE
**Answer:** What word formed in his mind from contemplating that "neat leg"?—"ELEGANT"

31. **Jumbles:** KHAKI PORGY JOCKEY TOWARD
**Answer:** What kids never play in school—HOOKY

32. **Jumbles:** YODEL GAWKY OUTCRY JOYOUS
**Answer:** Put this on a horse that's expected to win—A GOOD JOCKEY

33. **Jumbles:** BRAVO NUTTY EMERGE HUNGRY
**Answer:** He made every minute count, which is why they called him this—"MAN OF THE HOUR"

34. **Jumbles:** FIORD INEPT MODERN NUMBER
**Answer:** When the ship is in the harbor, the men in port might be this—"PROMINENT"

35. **Jumbles:** GIVEN FETCH CANYON ARCADE
**Answer:** Again in Paris!—"ENCORE!"

36. **Jumbles:** LURID IRONY KENNEL MILDEW
**Answer:** What a face drawn with care might be—WRINKLED

37. **Jumbles:** SMOKY PARTY HAIRDO LIQUOR
**Answer:** What he did when the doctor suggested he try some weight lifting—STOOD UP

38. **Jumbles:** SKUNK JETTY ABUSED BRANCH
**Answer:** Back in the Navy—STERN

39. **Jumbles:** STUNG THYME ANYONE INCOME
**Answer:** "Why not join us if you've" —NOTHING ON

40. **Jumbles:** GNARL FORUM HECTIC BRIDGE
**Answer:** Hands out money "right and left" but doesn't know how to spend it—RIGHT

41. **Jumbles:** CYCLE FLUID DUPLEX EYELID
**Answer:** What you might do when you no longer want your bike—"PEDDLE" IT

42. **Jumbles:** ICING FAUNA NATURE ORATOR
**Answer:** A monogamist doesn't believe in belonging to more than this—ONE UNION

43. **Jumbles:** TROTH RODEO CASKET DAINTY
**Answer:** What you have to face if you expect to learn how to drive safely—AHEAD

44. **Jumbles:** MAGIC BULLY GIBBET HOOKUP
**Answer:** What to do if you don't like granulated sugar in your coffee—LUMP IT

45. **Jumbles:** SHYLY BEFOG LATEST PURPLE
**Answer:** What jokes told by an abdominal surgeon are apt to be—BELLY LAUGHS

46. **Jumbles:** GIANT CLOTH ENCAMP SURTAX
**Answer:** The artist went to the picture frame shop because he has so many of these—HANG-UPS

47. **Jumbles:** WEIGH EXUDE VERSUS FROZEN
**Answer:** Why she liked the guy who always brought stale bread—HE NEVER GOT "FRESH"

48. **Jumbles:** DAISY AWARD DITHER FABLED
**Answer:** Which side of the fire is the hottest?—THE "FIRE SIDE"

49. **Jumbles:** ARMOR BRASS NEGATE SUBURB
**Answer:** What a backseat driver never does, unfortunately—RUNS OUT OF "GAS"

50. **Jumbles:** RUSTY NEWSY BOBBIN POETRY
**Answer:** His sandwich arrived squashed because he told the waiter to do this—"STEP ON IT"

51. **Jumbles:** AWASH NUTTY HIDING TIMELY
**Answer:** What's the first thing you see after looking for something in the dark?—THE LIGHT

52. **Jumbles:** ENJOY MAXIM GRUBBY MOSQUE
**Answer:** What they called that big silent elephant—A "MUM-BO JUMBO"

53. **Jumbles:** POUND GUIDE FONDLY EXCISE
**Answer:** What he did when he got that big gas bill—EXPLODED

54. **Jumbles:** SMOKY BARGE APATHY MUFFIN
**Answer:** What the frustrated actor turned butcher knew how to do—HAM IT UP

55. **Jumbles:** KNACK SWOOP LACKEY CROUCH
**Answer:** What kind of music do you get when you throw as stone in the water?— "PLUNK" ROCK

56. **Jumbles:** PROXY HEFTY BALLAD FUNGUS
**Answer:** What she said when her rejected suitor threatened to jump off the cliff—THAT'S ONLY A "BLUFF"

57. **Jumbles:** CYNIC AGING HEARSE SNITCH
**Answer:** He had no problem keeping up his end of the conversation, but a lot of trouble doing this—REACHING IT

58. **Jumbles:** FAULT BOUGH EFFACE GHETTO
**Answer:** You'll never lose weight if you try to do no more than this—LAUGH IT OFF

59. **Jumbles:** BRAWL EVENT TUSSLE STYMIE
**Answer:** With this kind of work, the model never seemed to feel fatigue—"AT-TIRELESS"

60. **Jumbles:** BULGY SKUNK LEEWAY AROUSE
**Answer:** What the carpenter who misplaced his tools was—A "SAW" LOSER

61. **Jumbles:** UNITY SAUTE QUENCH CASKET
**Answer:** Some people get what they want because they have this—THE "TAKE-NIQUE"

62. **Jumbles:** TITLE CLOAK SICKEN FITFUL
**Answer:** What he got when he took karate lessons—A KICK OUT OF IT

63. **Jumbles:** FEVER ENACT INFECT REALTY
**Answer:** Why they avoided the latest diet fad—IT WAS FACT FREE

64. **Jumbles:** TAKEN AGING ACTING OBLIGE
**Answer:** When he applied for the mortgage, the lender said he could—BANK ON IT

65. **Jumbles:** TRULY BRINY OSSIFY ZEALOT
**Answer:** After a day's work, the apple pickers showed the—FRUITS OF THEIR LABOR

66. **Jumbles:** KITTY SCARY COUSIN DISOWN
**Answer:** When he hung the drapes wrong, his boss said—"IT'S CURTAINS"

67. **Jumbles:** LIMBO ITCHY UTMOST FIESTA
**Answer:** What the TV repairman got from the irate customer—LOTS OF "STATIC"

68. **Jumbles:** BUXOM TULLE PAYING BEWAIL
**Answer:** Where the cowboy practiced for the big game—IN THE "BULL PEN"

69. **Jumbles:** YACHT MERGE KITTEN HERMIT
**Answer:** How he described his bout with insomnia—A NIGHTMARE

70. **Jumbles:** ROUSE CYNIC BUZZER INJURY
**Answer:** Frequently dropping in on a hot day—ICE CUBES

71. **Jumbles:** PAGAN CUBIC PARITY INHALE
**Answer:** What do you call a model turned seamstress?—A PIN-UP GIRL

72. **Jumbles:** LILAC LIGHT CASHEW THWART
**Answer:** Easy to tell on Halloween—WHICH IS WITCH

73. **Jumbles:** FACET NEWLY FABRIC GALAXY
**Answer:** Where you'll land if you try to bribe a cop—IN A REAL "FIX"

74. **Jumbles:** BOUGH FOYER SINFUL AMBUSH
**Answer:** What the young artist hoped for when he bought his supplies—A "BRUSH" WITH FAME

75. **Jumbles:** RAINY FETID SWERVE BOUGHT
**Answer:** When the trainee sold her 5 pairs of heels, the boss said he was—A SHOE-IN

76. **Jumbles:** SAUTE GASSY RARITY ALIGHT
**Answer:** What he did when he had one too many—SAT "TIGHT"

77. **Jumbles:** ORBIT WIPED POETIC TARTAR
**Answer:** When the vacationer stumbled while sightseeing, he said it was—A TRIP TRIP

78. **Jumbles:** BRAVO POWER ADMIRE BELLOW
**Answer:** A snag left the fisherman with this—A "REEL" PROBLEM

79. **Jumbles:** TRAIT HASTY BLEACH TURTLE
**Answer:** Easy to do when the sarge isn't looking—"STRETCH" THE TRUTH

80. **Jumbles:** RAVEN BULGY CASKET PITIED
**Answer:** What the passengers formed while waiting to board the ship—A CRUISE "LINE"

81. **Jumbles:** BRASS TUNED NEEDLE PAYOFF
**Answer:** When the boxer liked to get up—BEFORE "TEN"

82. **Jumbles:** VILLA EXTOL PELVIS LANCER
**Answer:** What she received at the cosmetic counter—LIP SERVICE

83. **Jumbles:** GULLY APART FRIEZE MUFFLE
**Answer:** Why he stopped at the gas station—TO "FILL UP"

84. **Jumbles:** COLON WHILE MIDWAY SALOON
**Answer:** What the instructor gave the divers before they entered the water—THE "LOWDOWN"

85. **Jumbles:** PLUME STOKE DONKEY FAULTY
**Answer:** How the pianist felt before his debut performance—ALL "KEYED" UP

86. **Jumbles:** FAUNA RHYME ALWAYS STOLID
**Answer:** What the couple acquired when they bought a cabin cruiser—A HOUSE FOR "SAIL"

87. **Jumbles:** CAPON TRILL JIGGER MYSTIC
**Answer:** When the players won the big game, they had—TEAM "SPIRIT"

88. **Jumbles:** TABOO LINER ENSIGN VOYAGE
**Answer:** This improved when the optometrist's office was remodeled—HIS EYE SITE

89. **Jumbles:** LITHE BAGGY LACING TWINGE
**Answer:** Experienced by most when put on hold—CALL, WAITING

90. **Jumbles:** CRAZE HAIRY BAKING DOOMED
**Answer:** What the dealer on the gambling boat was known as—A DECK HAND

91. **Jumbles:** DAISY HOBBY FORKED WEAKEN
**Answer:** Why the fisherman bought the new lure—HE WAS HOOKED

92. **Jumbles:** GUISE GLOAT MATRON GROUCH
**Answer:** What she showed when she stopped dyeing her hair—HER TRUE COLORS

93. **Jumbles:** USURY NOISE GAMBIT SIPHON
**Answer:** Hard to digest after a big meal—BORING HOSTS

94. **Jumbles:** JUROR YODEL INTENT PLURAL
**Answer:** What the bully did when he got into a "jam"—TURNED INTO JELLY

95. **Jumbles:** FABLE ROACH DETACH TRYING
**Answer:** What she gave her dieting husband when he had a midnight snack—A "FAT" CHANCE

96. **Jumbles:** MERCY FAULT DEPICT STUCCO
**Answer:** Where the photographer ended up when he ran into his girlfriend—OUT OF THE PICTURE

97. **Jumbles:** INLET SORRY DEFINE DAMASK
**Answer:** What the couple became when they opened a shoe repair shop—"SOLE" MATES

98. **Jumbles:** TARRY ICILY TERROR LIMPID
**Answer:** A farmer can turn a field into this—PAYDIRT

99. **Jumbles:** POISE LATCH BEFOUL MANAGE
**Answer:** What the tow truck driver tried to do when the sports car broke down—PULL A "FAST ONE"

100. **Jumbles:** BEGOT EJECT HIDING VENDOR
**Answer:** Where the high-rise riveter preferred working—ON THE EDGE

101. **Jumbles:** GNARL TWINE RADIUS PALATE
**Answer:** How they drove to their school reunion—IN THE "PAST" LANE

102. **Jumbles:** HELLO SIEGE PRIMED EIGHTY
**Answer:** What Junior turned into after he saw the monster movie—A "LIGHT" SLEEPER

103. **Jumbles:** AFOOT RUMMY DEFACE STIGMA
**Answer:** What she did to her budget when she went on a diet—TRIMMED THE FAT

104. **Jumbles:** CABLE PHOTO RANCOR IMMUNE
**Answer:** This was between the salesman and his good customer—THE COUNTER

105. **Jumbles:** UNWED WAGON KNOTTY CUDDLE
**Answer:** Received by the student pilot before his first landing—THE "LOWDOWN"

106. **Jumbles:** BATHE JOKER CAMPER HYBRID
**Answer:** What the sweaty cowboy did on a hot day—RODE "BAREBACK"

107. **Jumbles:** MILKY MIRTH MADMAN LEEWAY
**Answer:** How he felt when he walked in on his wife's sewing circle—"HEMMED" IN

108. **Jumbles:** GUMBO TARDY SHERRY BLOUSE
**Answer:** What the tipsy sailors faced when they returned from leave—A "SEA" OF TROUBLE

109. **Jumbles:** ELUDE FAMED FRIGID TUMULT
**Answer:** When the fortune teller went shopping, the saleslady said she was—A MEDIUM

110. **Jumbles:** ROBIN FISHY CONVEX HUNGRY
**Answer:** What the Paris musicians listened to on the road—FRENCH HORNS

111. **Jumbles:** CARGO NOBEL ENTAIL PLOWED
**Answer:** What the hairdresser did when the customer complained—BLEW HER TOP

112. **Jumbles:** CLOTH SEIZE NAUGHT STRONG
**Answer:** Where she was willing to go to change her width—TO GREAT "LENGTHS"

113. **Jumbles:** GUILT SNARL GENTLE IMPAIR
**Answer:** What the director considered the lighting expert's suggestion—ILLUMINATING

114. **Jumbles:** AWFUL DOILY ADVICE TIDBIT
**Answer:** The farm hand went to college to get this—"CULTIVATED"

115. **Jumbles:** FAITH PENCE DIVERT HALVED
**Answer:** The down-to-earth shopper bought the dresses because they were—DIRT CHEAP

116. **Jumbles:** JOLLY ESSAY SADIST MUFFIN
**Answer:** What the candidate's "sound" plan turned into—JUST NOISE

117. **Jumbles:** OXIDE DANDY SHEKEL DAINTY
**Answer:** How the manicurist made money—"HAND-ILY"

118. **Jumbles:** CABIN DEITY PENCIL BECOME
**Answer:** What the mob boss said when he was arrested—"I'M CONNECTED"

119. **Jumbles:** GOUGE OLDER CENSUS WIDEST
**Answer:** What Mom tied up on Christmas Eve—LOOSE ENDS

120. **Jumbles:** FORTY NAÏVE DELUXE CUDGEL
**Answer:** How the new vendor felt when he lost the balloons—DEFLATED

121. **Jumbles:** FEWER AFTER FIRING INTONE
**Answer:** What the aging mechanic considered while changing the balding wheels—"RE-TIRING"

122. **Jumbles:** DERBY YOUTH NEWEST TUXEDO
**Answer:** Why the friends argued at the boxing match—THEY WERE AT ODDS

123. **Jumbles:** PUDGY SHEEP SQUIRM PETITE
**Answer:** What the fancy new shoes did to the vagrant—TRIPPED HIM UP

124. **Jumbles:** HITCH PANSY EXHORT QUEASY
**Answer:** How the herder's helper felt when he lost the lambs—"SHEEPISH"

125. **Jumbles:** DELVE GUIDE INLAND DROWSY
**Answer:** Late-night studying with a snack made him this—WELL "ROUNDED"

126. **Jumbles:** TIGER CHALK WAYLAY AROUSE
**Answer:** What the clowns ended up with at the circus finale—THE LAST LAUGH

127. **Jumbles:** BROOD LOWLY AWHILE ASTHMA
**Answer:** When a piece was missing from her cake, Mom said his denial was—HARD TO SWALLOW

128. **Jumbles:** DUSKY PLUSH EROTIC IODINE
**Answer:** What the busy worker did when he grabbed a fast hot dog—HE "RELISHED" IT

129. **Jumbles:** NOVEL GRIPE BOBBIN MUSCLE
**Answer:** Saying good-bye to neighbors can be this—A "MOVING" SCENE

130. **Jumbles:** WHINE PILOT TONGUE BOTHER
**Answer:** What the dancers did during the ballet try-outs—WENT TOE TO TOE

131. **Jumbles:** LOVER APPLY DEAFEN UNLOCK
**Answer:** When Junior was grounded, he was left with this—A "PANED" LOOK

132. **Jumbles:** SKULK SNOWY MARVEL KIDNAP
**Answer:** Why the knife sharpener quit his job—IT'S DULL WORK

133. **Jumbles:** DUCAT COUGH ACCORD SINGLE
**Answer:** Often done by a helpful lathe operator—A GOOD "TURN"

134. **Jumbles:** RAPID YEARN DECEIT WEASEL
**Answer:** What she got when she bought that handbag—"CARRIED" AWAY

135. **Jumbles:** DRAFT WAFER EFFACE WHENCE
**Answer:** What the friends did when they ate their fast food lunch—CHEWED THE "FAT"

136. **Jumbles:** FRUIT HAVOC LEAVEN HOURLY
**Answer:** Where the beekeeper found himself when his honey sales tripled—IN THE "CLOVER"

137. **Jumbles:** LEAKY HABIT LAGOON BUTTON
**Answer:** He couldn't stop this when he quit smoking—TALKING ABOUT IT

138. **Jumbles:** GAILY PROBE MOBILE JUNKET
    **Answer:** What the fireworks crew did at the celebration—
    A "BANG" UP JOB

139. **Jumbles:** ERASE LURID OPENLY SHOULD
    **Answer:** Important for a garbage man to be—
    AT YOUR "DISPOSAL"

140. **Jumbles:** BRAWL SPURN DUPLEX STODGY
    **Answer:** A lot of whines come from this—SOUR GRAPES

141. **Jumbles:** EMERY BUSHY INVERT LAUNCH
    **Answer:** The organ grinder performed at the street festival
    when it was—HIS "TURN"

142. **Jumbles:** CAMEO FORCE DREDGE PURIFY
    **Answer:** What her ears felt like at the rock concert—
    "PIERCED"

143. **Jumbles:** FINIS MADLY FINITE PIGEON
    **Answer:** Why the novelist visited the cemetery—
    TO FIND "PLOTS"

144. **Jumbles:** ICING LEAVE TORRID BODICE
    **Answer:** How the orthopedist felt at the end of the day—
    "BONE" TIRED

145. **Jumbles:** LOUSE AVAIL IMBUED MYRIAD
    **Answer:** What the rock star became when he went on
    vacation—AN IDLE IDOL

146. **Jumbles:** POKED MOURN BEGONE LAWFUL
    **Answer:** How he looked on his wedding day—
    WELL "GROOMED"

147. **Jumbles:** CHIDE HUMAN BELONG MOTIVE
    **Answer:** When the judge made an error, his teammates said
    he belonged here—ON THE BENCH

148. **Jumbles:** MOUTH VIPER POSTAL SULTRY
    **Answer:** What the aviator became when he auditioned for a
    TV role—A TEST "PILOT"

149. **Jumbles:** VISOR TESTY EXHALE TACKLE
    **Answer:** This agent works here—A TAX "SHELTER"

150. **Jumbles:** HOUSE DOUGH CATTLE NAPKIN
    **Answer:** What the choirboy did when he was reprimanded
    for horseplay—CHANGED HIS "TUNE"

151. **Jumbles:** TACKY SOUSE MALICE GRASSY
    **Answer:** Barber students can do this without fear of
    penalty—CUT A CLASS

152. **Jumbles:** STUNG BEGUN OCCULT UPSHOT
    **Answer:** What Dad did with his new pest sprayer—
    GOT THE "BUGS" OUT

153. **Jumbles:** FEIGN RIGOR WEAPON COOKIE
    **Answer:** When he married for money, he ended up doing
    this—WORKING FOR IT

154. **Jumbles:** ONION GOING FINISH HYMNAL
    **Answer:** What he ended up doing when he went golfing—
    FISHING

155. **Jumbles:** EXCEL CLOUT FLORID THRASH
    **Answer:** This can lead to new opportunities in the push and
    pull of business—THE DOOR

156. **Jumbles:** QUAIL BUILT EASILY RATION
    **Answer:** A new mixer can create this—QUITE A STIR

157. **Jumbles:** EMPTY HUSKY INFUSE MARLIN
    **Answer:** What he reached when he completed the mountain
    race—HIS FITNESS "PEAK"

158. **Jumbles:** DITTO FINAL OXYGEN
    **Answer:** When the player worked hard to succeed, his coach
    said it was—"GOAL" TENDING

159. **Jumbles:** WHISK THICK DELUGE CALICO
    **Answer:** What the lad planned to do when he was as big as
    his father—LOSE WEIGHT

160. **Jumbles:** FANCY QUASH WHITEN WHALER
    **Answer:** He was determined to have sausages—IN THE
    "WURST" WAY

161. **Jumbles:** BRANCH UNPAID CANINE GALLEY HANGER
    CAUGHT
    **Answer:** The rain-soaked sentry looked forward to the—
    "CHANGING" OF THE GUARD

162. **Jumbles:** PACKET UPHELD GRIMLY VIRTUE FLEECE TYPING
    **Answer:** What big sister did while Mom got fitted for
    glasses—KEPT AN EYE ON HIM

163. **Jumbles:** DIGEST ICEBOX ORIGIN PLENTY SMUDGE SURETY
    **Answer:** The dancers returned to Ireland to get back to their
    old—STOMPING GROUNDS

164. **Jumbles:** AFLOAT BENIGN ISLAND FICKLE CIPHER EQUATE
    **Answer:** Making tea on a mountain climb can be a—
    "STEEP" CHALLENGE

165. **Jumbles:** ASYLUM DENTAL SUCKLE AFFIRM GRAVEN BEHELD
    **Answer:** Why he entered the knot-tying contest—
    TO MAKE ENDS MEET

166. **Jumbles:** HARBOR HERALD GOATEE WEEVIL CIRCUS
    FURROW
    **Answer:** Why she decided to start her diet immediately—
    THE WEIGHT WAS "OVER"

167. **Jumbles:** HELMET GOODLY TYCOON UNCLAD DITHER
    BAFFLE
    **Answer:** Enjoyed by a successful physician—
    A "HEALTHY" INCOME

168. **Jumbles:** WALNUT SUBURB ARTERY FORBID CAJOLE FACILE
    **Answer:** Needed by a ship's captain on an ocean voyage—
    CRUISE "CONTROL"

169. **Jumbles:** ACCENT DURESS ANYONE SUBDUE BODILY CLAUSE
    **Answer:** Often change hands at a perfume counter—
    DOLLARS AND SCENTS

170. **Jumbles:** GARLIC INDIGO GUNNER ANEMIA BOTANY SEXTON
    **Answer:** What the voice student did when the bank was
    robbed—HE BEGAN "SINGING"

171. **Jumbles:** OBTUSE THEORY PANTRY BANNER MATURE INFIRM
    **Answer:** When the buyer was refused a refund, he was at
    the—POINT OF "NO RETURN"

172. **Jumbles:** ALBINO FALLEN MULISH CAMPUS PLACID BANTER
    **Answer:** The well-dressed ladies ate off designer dishes
    because they were—"FASHION" PLATES

173. **Jumbles:** UNHOOK DILUTE RADIUM FROLIC PREACH STUPID
    **Answer:** The housemaid was fired because she—
    LACKED "POLISH"

174. **Jumbles:** EXODUS MISUSE POLICE SNUGLY AFRAID FINERY
    **Answer:** What the laundry faced when the shirt came back
    wrinkled—A "PRESSING" ISSUE

175. **Jumbles:** ARCADE FEEBLE TANDEM ERMINE PURVEY
    POMADE
    **Answer:** What the fugitive said when he saw his "Wanted"
    poster—"I'VE BEEN FRAMED"

176. **Jumbles:** USEFUL FASTEN LOUNGE PEPTIC EXTENT PERSON
    **Answer:** When the banker gave himself a loan at a favorabe
    rate, it was—SELF "INTEREST"

177. **Jumbles:** TOUCHY COERCE OPAQUE BICKER TIPTOE APPEAR
    **Answer:** Using the switchboard to book bets made him
    this—QUITE AN "OPERATOR"

178. **Jumbles:** OCELOT TALLOW EMBODY FLURRY NOUGAT
    ADDUCE
    **Answer:** Why the teacher didn't mind when the test answers
    were shouted out—ALOUD WAS ALLOWED

179. **Jumbles:** REDUCE UNLOAD BLITHE ABUSED EXPOSE ORCHID
    **Answer:** When she wore a flimsy outfit on a cold night, she
    was—DRESSED TO "CHILL"

180. **Jumbles:** PIGPEN UNHOLY SEETHE ANGINA MOSAIC QUARTZ
    **Answer:** What the nervous groom didn't have on his
    wedding day—A "SINGLE" THOUGHT

# Need More Jumbles®?

Order any of these books through your bookseller or call Triumph Books toll-free at 800-335-5323.

## Jumble® Books

**More than 175 puzzles each!**

**Animal Jumble®**
$9.95 • ISBN: 1-57243-197-0

**Jammin' Jumble®**
$9.95 • ISBN: 1-57243-844-4

**Jazzy Jumble®**
$9.95 • ISBN: 978-1-57243-962-7

**Jolly Jumble®**
$9.95 • ISBN: 978-1-60078-214-5

**Joyful Jumble®**
$9.95 • ISBN: 978-1-60078-079-0

**Jumble® at Work**
$9.95 • ISBN: 1-57243-147-4

**Jumble® Celebration**
$9.95 • ISBN: 978-1-60078-134-6

**Jumble® Explosion**
$9.95 • ISBN: 978-1-60078-078-3

**Jumble® Fever**
$9.95 • ISBN: 1-57243-593-3

**Jumble® Fiesta**
$9.95 • ISBN: 1-57243-626-3

**Jumble® Fun**
$9.95 • ISBN: 1-57243-379-5

**Jumble® Genius**
$9.95 • ISBN: 1-57243-896-7

**Jumble® Grab Bag**
$9.95 • ISBN: 1-57243-273-X

**Jumble® Jackpot**
$9.95 • ISBN: 1-57243-897-5

**Jumble® Jamboree**
$9.95 • ISBN: 1-57243-696-4

**Jumble® Jubilee**
$9.95 • ISBN: 1-57243-231-4

**Jumble® Juggernaut**
$9.95 • ISBN: 978-1-60078-026-4

**Jumble® Junction**
$9.95 • ISBN: 1-57243-380-9

**Jumble® Jungle**
$9.95 • ISBN: 978-1-57243-961-0

**Jumble® Madness**
$9.95 • ISBN: 1-892049-24-4

**Jumble® Mania**
$9.95 • ISBN: 1-57243-697-2

**Jumble® See & Search**
$9.95 • ISBN: 1-57243-549-6

**Jumble® See & Search 2**
$9.95 • ISBN: 1-57243-734-0

**Jumble® Surprise**
$9.95 • ISBN: 1-57243-320-5

**Jumble® Junction**
$9.95 • ISBN: 1-57243-380-9

**Jump, Jive and Jumble®**
$9.95 • ISBN: 978-1-60078-000-0

**Jumpin' Jumble®**
$9.95 • ISBN: 978-1-60078-027-1

**Ready, Set, Jumble®**
$9.95 • ISBN: 978-1-60078-133-0

**Sports Jumble®**
$9.95 • ISBN: 1-57243-113-X

**Summer Fun Jumble®**
$9.95 • ISBN: 1-57243-114-8

**Travel Jumble®**
$9.95 • ISBN: 1-57243-198-9

**TV Jumble®**
$9.95 • ISBN: 1-57243-461-9

## Oversize Jumble® Books

**More than 500 puzzles each!**

**Colossal Jumble®**
$19.95 • ISBN: 1-57243-490-2

**Generous Jumble®**
$19.95 • ISBN: 1-57243-385-X

**Giant Jumble®**
$19.95 • ISBN: 1-57243-349-3

**Gigantic Jumble®**
$19.95 • ISBN: 1-57243-426-0

**Jumbo Jumble®**
$19.95 • ISBN: 1-57243-314-0

**The Very Best of Jumble® BrainBusters**
$19.95 • ISBN: 1-57243-845-2

## Jumble® Crosswords™

**More than 175 puzzles each!**

**Jumble® Crosswords™**
$9.95 • ISBN: 1-57243-347-7

**More Jumble® Crosswords™**
$9.95 • ISBN: 1-57243-386-8

**Jumble® Crosswords™ Adventure**
$9.95 • ISBN: 1-57243-462-7

**Jumble® Crosswords™ Challenge**
$9.95 • ISBN: 1-57243-423-6

**Jumble® Crosswords™ Jackpot**
$9.95 • ISBN: 1-57243-615-8

**Jumble® Crosswords™ Jamboree**
$9.95 • ISBN: 1-57243-787-1

## Jumble® BrainBusters™

**More than 175 puzzles each!**

**Jumble® BrainBusters™**
$9.95 • ISBN: 1-892049-28-7

**Jumble® BrainBusters™ II**
$9.95 • ISBN: 1-57243-424-4

**Jumble® BrainBusters™ III**
$9.95 • ISBN: 1-57243-463-5

**Jumble® BrainBusters™ IV**
$9.95 • ISBN: 1-57243-489-9

**Jumble® BrainBusters™ 5**
$9.95 • ISBN: 1-57243-548-8

**Hollywood Jumble® BrainBusters™**
$9.95 • ISBN: 1-57243-594-1

**Jumble® BrainBusters™ Bonanza**
$9.95 • ISBN: 1-57243-616-6

**Boggle™ BrainBusters™**
$9.95 • ISBN: 1-57243-592-5

**Boggle™ BrainBusters™ 2**
$9.95 • ISBN: 1-57243-788-X

**Jumble® BrainBusters™ Junior**
$9.95 • ISBN: 1-892049-29-5

**Jumble® BrainBusters™ Junior II**
$9.95 • ISBN: 1-57243-425-2

**Fun in the Sun with Jumble® BrainBusters™**
$9.95 • ISBN: 1-57243-733-2